THE ARCHAEOLOGY
OF THE
CUNEIFORM INSCRIPTIONS

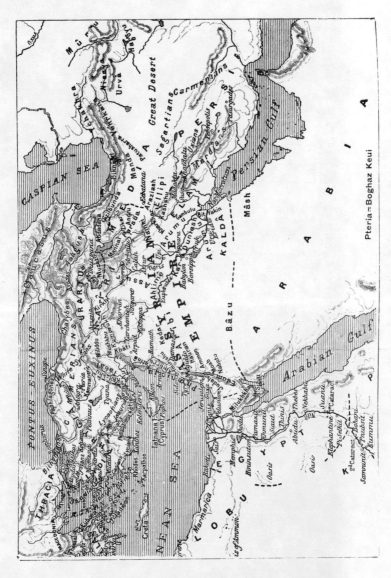

THE EASTERN WORLD IN THE SEVENTH CENTURY B.C.

Pteria=Boghaz Keui

THE ARCHAEOLOGY
OF THE
CUNEIFORM INSCRIPTIONS

By

REV. A.H. SAYCE

PROFESSOR OF ASSYRIOLOGY, OXFORD

ARES PUBLISHERS INC.
CHICAGO   MCMLXXVIII

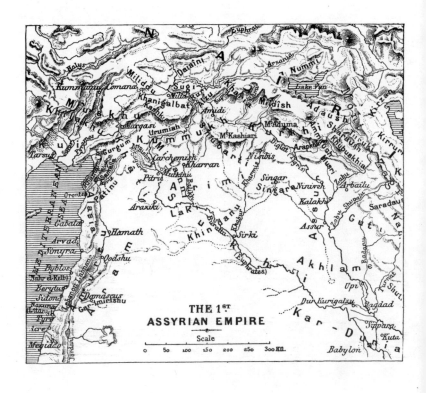

THE 1ST
ASSYRIAN EMPIRE

Scale

0   50   100   150   200   250   300 KИ.

Exact Reprint of the Edition:
London 1907
ARES PUBLISHERS, INC.
7020 NORTH WESTERN AVE.
CHICAGO, ILLINOIS 60645
Printed in the United States of America
International Standard Book Number:
0-89005-228-X

The Archæology of the Cuneiform Inscriptions

BY THE

Rev. A. H. SAYCE

PROFESSOR OF ASSYRIOLOGY, OXFORD

CONTENTS

PREFACE

THE first six chapters which follow, embody the Rhind Lectures in Archæology which I delivered at Edinburgh in October 1906. The seventh chapter appeared as an article in the *Contemporary Review* for August 1905, and is here reprinted by the courtesy of the Editor to whom I render my thanks. The book is the first attempt to deal with what I would call the archæology of cuneiform decipherment, and like all pioneering work consequently claims the indulgence of the reader. For the sake of clearness I have been forced to repeat myself in a few instances, more especially in the sixth chapter, but what has thereby been lost in literary finish will, I hope, be compensated by an increase of clearness in the argument.

If what I have written serves no other purpose, I shall be content if it draws attention to the miserably defective state of our archæological knowledge of Babylonia and Assyria, and to the necessity of scientific excavations being carried on there similar to those inaugurated by Mr. Rhind in Egypt. We have abundance of epigraphic material; it is the more purely archæological material that is still wanting.

The need of it is every year becoming more urgent with the ever-growing revelation of the important and far-reaching part played by Babylonian culture in the ancient East. Excavation is just commencing in Asia Minor, and there are many indications that it has startling discoveries and surprises in store for us. Even while my manuscript was in the printer's hands, Professor Winckler has been

examining the cuneiform tablets found by him last spring
at Boghaz Keui, on the site of the old Hittite capital in
Cappadocia, and reading in them the records of the Hittite
kings, Khattu-sil, Sapaluliuma, Mur-sila and Muttallu. Most
of the tablets, though written in cuneiform characters, are
in the native language of the country, but among them is
a version in the Babylonian language of the treaty between
the "great king of the Hittites" and Ramesa Miya-Amana
or Ramses II., the Egyptian copy of which has long been
known to us. The two Arzawan letters in the Tel el-
Amarna collection no longer stand alone; the Boghaz
Keui tablets show that an active correspondence was
carried on between Egypt and Cappadocia. We must
revise our old ideas about an absence of intercourse between
different parts of the ancient Oriental world : there was
quite as much intercommunication as there is to-day.
Elam and Babylonia, Assyria and Asia Minor, Palestine
and Egypt, all were linked together by the ties of a common
culture; there were no exclusive religions to raise barriers
between nation and nation, and the pottery of the Hittites
was not only carried to the south of Canaan, but the
civilization of Babylonia made its way through Hittite
lands to the shores and islands of Greece. On the south,
the Ægean became a highway from Asia Minor to Europe,
while northward the Troad formed a bridge which carried
the culture of Cappadocia to the Balkans and the Danube.

A. H. SAYCE.

November 1906.

THE ARCHÆOLOGY OF THE CUNEIFORM INSCRIPTIONS

CHAPTER I

THE DECIPHERMENT OF THE CUNEIFORM INSCRIPTIONS

THE decipherment of the cuneiform inscriptions was the archæological romance of the nineteenth century. There was no Rosetta stone to offer a clue to their meaning; the very names of the Assyrian kings and of the gods they worshipped had been lost and forgotten; and the characters themselves were but conventional groups of wedges, not pictures of objects and ideas like the hieroglyphs of Egypt. The decipherment started with the guess of a classical scholar who knew no Oriental languages and had never travelled in the East. And yet it is upon this guess that the vast superstructure of cuneiform decipherment has been slowly reared, with its ever-increasing mass of literature in numerous languages, the very existence of some of which had been previously unknown, and with its revelation of a civilized world that had faded out of sight before Greek history began. The ancient East has risen, as it were, from the dead, with its politics and its wars, its law and its trade, its art, its industries and its science. And this revelation of a new world, this resurrection of a dead past, has started from a successful guess. But the guess had been made in accordance with scientific method and had scientific reasons behind it, and it has proved to be the fruitful seed of an overspreading tree.

Seventy years ago a single small case was sufficient to hold all the Assyrian and Babylonian antiquities possessed by the British Museum. They had been collected by Rich, to whom we owe the first accurate plans of the sites of Babylon and Nineveh. But the cuneiform characters found on the seals and clay cylinders of Babylonia were not the only characters of the kind that were known. Similar characters had been noticed by travellers on the walls of the ruined palaces of Persepolis in Persia. As far back as 1621 the Italian traveller Pietro della Valle had copied two or three of these, which he reproduced in the account of his travels some thirty years later. One of the first acts of the newly-founded Royal Society of Great Britain was to ask in their *Philosophical Transactions* (p. 420) whether some draughtsman could not be found to copy the bas-reliefs and inscriptions which had thus been observed at Persepolis, though the only result of the inquiry was that a few years afterwards (in June 1693) two lines of cuneiform were published in the *Transactions* from the papers of a Mr. Samuel Flower, who had been the agent of the East India Company in Persia. The editor of the *Transactions* correctly concluded that the inscriptions were to be read from left to right. The cuneiform characters which were printed in the *Transactions* were, however, not the first specimens of cuneiform script that had been published in England. Thomas Herbert, in the fourth edition of his Travels, which appeared in 1677, had already given three lines of characters taken indifferently from the three classes of inscriptions engraved on the Persian monuments ; these were afterwards annexed by an Italian named Careri, who published them as his own. But the earliest inscription to be reproduced in full was a short one inscribed by Darius I. over the windows of his palace, which had been copied by Sir John Chardin during one of his two visits to Persepolis (in 1665 and 1673). Chardin was the son of a Huguenot jeweller in Paris, and after returning from his travels settled in London, where he became a great favourite of Charles II., and was made a Fellow of the Royal Society. The inscription. he had copied, however, was not printed in the earlier edition of his Travels, and had to wait until 1735 before it saw the light.[1]

The existence of the cuneiform script thus became known in Europe, and that was all. It was not until Carsten Niebuhr, the father of the better-known historian, had been sent by the Danish Government on an exploring mission to the East that fairly complete and accurate copies of the inscriptions of Persepolis were at last put into the hands of European scholars. Niebuhr, who sacrificed his sight to the work, returned to Denmark in 1767, and seven years later the first of the three volumes in which the scientific results of his

---

[1] In this year an elaborate edition of his work was brought out under the title of *Voyages du Chevalier Chardin en Perse, et autres Lieux de l'Orient, Enrichis de Figures en Tailledouce, qui représentent les Antiquités et les Choses remarquables du Païs* (Amsterdam), two pages (167-8) in vol. ii. being devoted to the inscriptions, the cuneiform being printed on plate lxix.

travels were embodied was published at Copenhagen.
With the publication of the second volume, which
contained his description of the Persepolitan monuments, the attempt to decipher the cuneiform characters began. He himself had noticed that in the first
of the three classes or systems of cuneiform writing
of which every inscription consisted, only forty-two
characters were employed, and he therefore concluded
that the system was alphabetic. Another Dane,
Bishop Münter, discovered that the words in it were
divided from one another by an oblique wedge,[1] and
further showed that the monuments must belong to
the age of Cyrus and his successors.[2] One word,
which occurs without any variation towards the beginning of each inscription, he correctly inferred to
signify "king"; but beyond this he was unable to
advance.

Meanwhile, Anquetil-Duperron, with self-sacrificing
enthusiasm, had rediscovered the Zend of the later
Zoroastrian faith, and de Sacy, with the help of it, had
deciphered the Pehlevi inscriptions of the Sassanid
kings. It was only the older Persian of the Achæmenian cuneiform inscriptions that still awaited interpretation; and a bridge had been built between it and
modern Persian by means of the Zendic texts. In
1802 the guess was made which opened the way to
the decipherment of the mysterious wedge-shaped
signs. The inspired genius was Grotefend, an accom-

[1] The discovery has sometimes been claimed for Tychsen
(*De cuneatis Inscriptionibus Persepolitanis Lucubratio*, 1798,
p. 24), but Tychsen supposed that the wedge was used to divide
sentences, not words.
[2] *Undersögelser om de Persepolitanske Inscriptioner* (1800),
translated into German in 1802.

plished Latinist and a school-master at Frankfort-on-the-Main. He knew no Oriental languages, but his mother-wit and common-sense more than made up for the deficiency. It was clear to him that the three systems of cuneiform represented three different languages, the Persian kings being like a Turkish pasha of to-day, who, when he wishes an edict to be understood, writes it in Turkish and Arabic. It was also clear to him that the first system must be the script of the Persian kings themselves, of which the other two were translations. The preparatory work for reading this had already been done by Münter ; what Grotefend now had to do was to identify and read the names to which the word for "king" was attached.

On comparing the inscriptions together he found that while the word for "king" remained unchanged, the word which accompanied it at the beginning of an inscription varied on different monuments. There were, in fact, two wholly different words, one of which was peculiar to one set of monuments, the other to another set. But he also found that the first of these words followed the other on the second set of monuments, though with a different termination from that which belonged to it when it took the place of the first word. Hence he conjectured that the two words represented the names of two Persian kings, one of whom was the son of the other, the termination of the second name when it followed the first being that of the genitive. It was now necessary to discover who the kings were whose names had thus been found. Fortunately the Achæmenian dynasty was not a long one, and the number of royal names in it was not large. And of these names, Cyrus was too short and

Artaxerxes too long for either of the two names which Grotefend had detected. There only remained Darius and Xerxes, and as Xerxes was the son of Darius, the name which characterized the first set of monuments must be Darius.

Grotefend's next task was to ascertain the old Persian pronunciation of the name of Darius. This had been given by Strabo, while the Persian pronunciation of Xerxes was indicated in the Old Testament. With this assistance Grotefend was able to assign alphabetic values to the cuneiform characters which composed the two names, and a corner of the veil which had so long covered the cuneiform records was lifted at last. A comparison of the names which he had thus read gave the needful verification of the correctness of his method. In the names of Darius and Xerxes the same letters occur, but in different places ; *a* and *r* in *Darius* occupy the second and third places, in *Xerxes* the fourth and fifth, while *sh*, which is the last letter in *Darius*, would be the second and sixth in *Xerxes*. And such was actually the case. Grotefend was therefore justified in concluding that his guesses were correct, and that the right values had been assigned to the cuneiform characters. A beginning had been made in cuneiform decipherment, and in this instance the beginning was half the whole.

Grotefend's Memoir was presented to the Göttingen Academy on September 4, 1802. By a curious accident it was at the same meeting that Heyne described the first attempts that had been made towards deciphering the Egyptian hieroglyphs. But the learned world looked askance at the discoveries of the young Latinist. The science of archæology was still unborn, and Oriental philologists were unable even to understand the inductive method of the decipherer. The Academy of Göttingen refused to print his communications, and it was not until 1815 that they appeared in the first volume of the History of his friend Heeren, who, being untrammelled by the prejudices of Oriental learning, had been one of the earliest to accept his conclusions.[1] For a whole generation the work of decipherment was allowed to sleep.

It is unfortunately true that after his initial success Grotefend's ignorance of Oriental languages really did stand in his way. He assumed that the language of the inscriptions and that of the *Zend-Avesta* were one and the same, and accordingly went to the newly-found Zend dictionary for the readings of the cuneiform names and words. Vishtaspa, the name of the father of Darius, was thus read Goshtasp, the word for "king" became *khsheh* instead of *khshayathiya*, and that which Grotefend had correctly divined to signify "great," *eghre* instead of *vazraka*. It is not wonderful, therefore, that he was never able to follow up the beginning he had made.

[1] *Ideen über die Politik, den Verkehr und den Handel der vornehmsten Völker der alten Welt,* vol. i. pp. 563 *sqq.* ; translated into English in 1833. The revival of interest in Grotefend's work was due to the fact that Champollion, after the decipherment of the Egyptian hieroglyphs, found the name of Xerxes on an alabaster vase at Paris on which, according to Grotefend's system, the same name was written in Persian cuneiform. This led the Abbé Saint-Martin, who was a recognized Orientalist, to adopt and follow up Grotefend's discovery in a Memoir which he read before the French Academy in 1822, and Saint-Martin's work attracted the attention of Rask and Burnouf.

To do this was reserved for the Zendic scholars of a later generation. Rask the Dane in 1826 determined the true form of the genitive plural, and thereby identified the character for *m* which gave him the names of the supreme god Auramazda and of Achæmenes the forefather of Cyrus.[1] But the great step forward was made by the eminent French scholar, Emile Burnouf, in 1836.[2] The first of the inscriptions published by Niebuhr he discovered to contain a list of the satrapies of Darius. With this clue in his hand the reading of the names and the subsequent identification of the letters which composed them could be a question only of patience and time. For this Burnouf was well equipped by his philological knowledge and training, and the result was an alphabet of thirty letters, the greater part of which had been correctly deciphered.

Burnouf's Memoir on the subject was published in June 1836. In the preceding month his friend and pupil, Professor Lassen of Bonn, had also published a work on " The Old Persian Cuneiform Inscriptions of Persepolis."[3] He and Burnouf had been in frequent correspondence, and his claim to have independently detected the names of the satrapies, and thereby to have fixed the values of the Persian characters, was in consequence fiercely attacked. To the attacks made upon him, however, Lassen never vouchsafed a reply. Whatever his obligations to Burnouf may have been,

[1] "Om Zendsprogets," in the *Skandinaviske Literaturselskabs Skrifter*, xxi., translated into German in 1826.
[2] *Mémoire sur deux Inscriptions cunéiformes trouvées près d'Hamadan* (Paris, 1836).
[3] *Die Altpersischen Keil-Inschriften von Persepolis* (Bonn, 1836).

his own contributions to the decipherment of the inscriptions were numerous and important. He succeeded in fixing the true values of nearly all the letters in the Persian alphabet, in translating the texts, and in proving that the language of them was not Zend, but stood to both Zend and Sanskrit in the relation of a sister.

Meanwhile another scholar, armed with fresh and important material, had entered the field. A young English officer in the East India Company's service, Major Rawlinson by name, was attached to the British Mission in Persia. A happy inspiration led him to attempt the decipherment of the cuneiform inscriptions. It was in 1835, when he was twenty-five years old, that he first began his work. All that he knew was that Grotefend had discovered in the texts of Persepolis the names of Darius, of Xerxes and of Hystaspes, but cut off as he was in his official position at Kirmanshah on the western frontier of Persia from European libraries, he was unable to procure either the Memoir of the German scholar or the articles to which it had given rise. Like Burnouf, he set himself to decipher the two inscriptions of Hamadan, which he had himself copied with great care. He soon recognized in them the names that had been read by Grotefend, and thus obtained a working alphabet. But his position in Persia soon gave him an advantage which was denied to his fellow-workers in Europe. It was not long before he found an opportunity of copying the great inscription on the sacred rock of Behistun, which had never been copied before. It was by far the longest cuneiform inscription yet discovered, and was filled with proper names, including those of the Persian satrapies. The copying of it, however, cost much time and labour, and was accomplished at actual risk of life, as Major Rawlinson, better known by his later title of Sir Henry Rawlinson, had to be lowered in a basket from the top of the cliff in order to ascertain the exact forms of certain characters.

In the following year (1836) Rawlinson moved to Teheran, and there received from Edwin Norris, the Secretary of the Royal Asiatic Society, the Memoirs of Grotefend and Saint-Martin. In 1837 he finished his copy of the Behistun inscription, and sent a translation of its opening paragraphs to the Royal Asiatic Society. Before, however, his Paper could be published, the works of Lassen and Burnouf reached him, necessitating a revision of his Paper and the postponement of its publication. Then came other causes of delay. He was called away to Afghanistan to perform the onerous and responsible duties of British Agent at Kandahar, and it was not until 1843 that he was once more free to resume his cuneiform studies. A year later he was visited by the Danish Professor, Westergaard, who placed at his disposal the copies he had just made of the inscription on the tomb of Darius at Naksh-i-Rustam and of some shorter inscriptions from Persepolis, and Rawlinson's Memoir was accordingly finished at last and sent to England. Here Norris subjected it to a careful revision, and at his suggestion Rawlinson once more visited Behistun, where he took squeezes and re-examined doubtful characters. In 1847 the first part of the Memoir was published, though the second part, containing the analysis and commentary on the text, did not appear

CHALDÆAN HOUSEHOLD UTENSILS IN
TERRA-COTTA.

[*See p.* 52.

BLACK OBELISK OF SHAL-
MANESER II.

[*See p.* 21.

THE SEAL OF SHARGANI-SHAR-ALI (SARGON OF AKKAD): GILGAMES WATERS
THE CELESTIAL OX.

BAS-RELIEF OF NARAM-SIN.

SITTING STATUE OF GUDEA.

THE TOMB OF DARIUS.

till 1849.[1] The work, however, was well worthy of the time and care that had been bestowed upon it. The task of deciphering the Persian cuneiform texts was virtually accomplished, and the guesses of Grotefend had developed into the discovery of a new alphabet and a new language. The capstone was put to the work by the discovery of Hincks, an Irish clergyman, that the alphabet was not a true one in the modern sense of the word, a vowel-sound being attached in pronunciation to each of the consonants represented in it.

The mystery of the Persian cuneiform texts was thus solved after nearly fifty years of endeavour. A harder task still remained. The Persian texts were accompanied by two other cuneiform transcripts, which, as Grotefend had perceived, must have represented the other two principal languages that were spoken in the Persian Empire. That the third transcript was Babylonian seemed evident from the resemblance of the characters contained in it to those on the bricks and seal-cylinders of Babylonia. Grotefend had already written upon the subject, and had even divined the name of Nebuchadrezzar on certain Babylonian bricks.

But this third species of writing, which we must henceforth term Babylonian or Assyrian, presented extraordinary difficulties. Instead of an alphabet of forty-two letters, the decipherer was confronted by an enormous number of different characters, while no indication was given of the separation of one word from another. Moreover the forms of the characters as found on the Persepolitan monuments differed

<hr />

[1] *Journal of the Royal Asiatic Society*, x.

considerably from those found on the Babylonian monuments, which again differed greatly from each other. On the seal-cylinders, more especially, they assumed the most complicated shapes, between which and the Persepolitan forms it was often impossible to trace any likeness whatever.

Suddenly a discovery was made which furnished an abundance of new material and incited the decipherer to fresh efforts. In 1842 Botta was sent to Mossul as French Consul, and at Mohl's instigation began to excavate on the site of Nineveh. His first essays there not proving very successful, he transferred his workmen further north, to the mound of Khorsabad, and there laid bare the ruins of a large and splendid palace which subsequently turned out to be that of Sargon. In the autumn of 1845 the excavations of Botta were succeeded by those of Layard, first at Nimrûd (the ancient Calah), and then at Kûyunjik or Nineveh, the result being to fill the British Museum with bas-reliefs covered with cuneiform writing and with other relics of Assyrian civilization.

The inscriptions brought to light by Botta were copied and published by him in 1846–50.[1] The sumptuous work which was dedicated to them was followed by a smaller and cheaper edition, and the author gave further help to the student by classifying the characters, which amounted to as many as 642.[2] His work proved conclusively the identity of the script used at Nineveh with that of the third tran-

---

[1] *Monument de Ninive*, with plates drawn by Flandin.
[2] See his Memoir, " Sur l'écriture assyrienne," in the *Journal asiatique*, 1847–8, ix.-xi.

scripts on the Persian monuments, as well as the substantial agreement of the groups of characters occurring in each.

The Irish scholar Dr. Hincks—one of the most remarkable and acute decipherers that have ever lived —was already at work on the newly-found texts. In 1847 he published a long article on "The Three Kinds of Persepolitan Writing,"[1] and, two years later, another, "On the Khorsabad Inscriptions."[2] In 1850 he read a Paper before the British Association,[3] summing up his conclusions and announcing the important discovery that the Assyrian characters were syllabic and not alphabetic, as had hitherto been supposed. With this discovery the scientific decipherment of the Assyrian inscriptions actually begins.

The proper names contained in the Persian texts furnished the clue to the reading of the Babylonian transcripts. The values thus obtained for the Babylonian characters made it possible to read many of the words, the meaning of which was fixed by a comparison with the Persian original. It then became clear that Assyrian was a Semitic language, standing in much the same relation to Hebrew that the Old Persian stood to Zend.

Its Semitic origin was proved to demonstration by the French scholar de Saulcy in 1849. Another French scholar, de Longpérier, had already discovered the name of Sargon in the Khorsabad inscriptions[4]— the first royal Assyrian name that had yet been read.

[1] *Transactions of the Royal Irish Academy*, xxi. pp. 240 *sqq.* See also pp. 114 *sqq.*
[2] *Transactions of the Royal Irish Academy*, xxii. pp. 3 *sqq.*
[3] Edinburgh Meeting, p. 140.
[4] *Revue archéologique*, 1847, pp. 501 *sqq.*

De Saulcy himself subjected the Babylonian transcript of the trilingual inscription of Elwend to a minute analysis, and so carefully was the work performed, and so secure were the foundations upon which it rested, that the translation needs but little revision even to-day.[1] The old belief in the alphabetic nature of the characters, however, still possessed the mind of the decipherer, although in one passage he goes so far as to say, " I am tempted to believe " that the signs are syllabic. But he did not go beyond the temptation to believe, and the discovery was reserved for Hincks.

Rawlinson was now at Bagdad. De Saulcy sent him his Memoirs, and the British scholar had the immense advantage of having in his hands the Babylonian version of the great Behistun inscription, of knowing the country in which the monuments were found, and of possessing copies of inscriptions which had not yet made their way to Europe.

Nevertheless, it is amazing with what rapidity and perspicacity he forced his way through the thick jungle of cuneiform script. In his Memoir on the Persian texts, published in 1847, he already maps out with marvellous fulness and exactitude the different varieties of cuneiform writing. It is his second Memoir, however, which excites in the Assyriologist of to-day the profoundest feelings of surprise and admiration. This consists of notes on the inscriptions of Assyria and Babylonia, and was communicated to the Royal Asiatic Society at the beginning of the year 1850.[2]

---

[1] *Recherches sur l'écriture cunéiforme assyrienne* (1849).
[2] *Journal of the Royal Asiatic Society*, xii. pp. 401 *sqq.* The translation of the Black Obelisk inscription is given on pp. 431–48.

One of the inscriptions he has translated in full—the annals of Shalmaneser II., on an obelisk of black marble discovered at Nimrûd and now in the British Museum. The text is a long one, and for the first time the European reader had placed before him a contemporaneous account of the campaigns of an Assyrian monarch in the ninth century before our era. The translation is substantially correct; it is only in the proper names that Rawlinson has gone much astray. The values of many of the characters were still uncertain or unknown, and he was under the domination of the belief that they represented alphabetic letters.

He was, moreover, mistaken as to the age of the monument itself, which he assigned to too early an epoch. It was Dr. Hincks who again settled the question, by reading upon it the names of Hazael of Damascus and Jehu of Israel.[1] This was one of the first-fruits of his discovery of the syllabic character of the Assyrian signs. Another was the discovery of the name of Sennacherib,[2] as well as those of Hezekiah and Jerusalem.[3]

Shortly before this Hincks had made another discovery of importance. He had deciphered the names of Nebuchadrezzar and his father on the bricks of Babylon,[4] and had further shown that a cylinder of Nebuchadrezzar brought from Babylon by Sir Robert Ker-Porter, and written in the cuneiform characters met with on the Persian monuments, contained the

[1] *Athenæum*, December 27, 1851.
[2] In the Paper read by Hincks before the Royal Irish Academy in June 1849, and published the following year.
[3] For Hincks's translation of the annals of Sennacherib, see Layard's *Nineveh and Babylon*, pp. 139 *sqq.*
[4] *Literary Gazette*, July 5, 1846.

same text as another cylinder obtained by Sir Harford
Jones, and inscribed with characters of the most
complex kind. A comparison of the two texts gave
him the values of the latter characters, which we now
know to represent the archaic Babylonian forms of
the cuneiform signs.

But the decipherment of the Assyro-Babylonian
script was not yet complete. In 1851 Rawlinson's
long-promised Memoir on the Babylonian version
of the inscription of Behistun was given to the world,[1]
and consisted of the cuneiform text, with translation,
grammar and commentary, besides a list of 242 characters. It announced, moreover, two facts about these
characters, one of which had already been recognized,
while the second was received by the Orientalists
with shouts of incredulity. The first fact was that the
characters, besides having phonetic values, could also
be used ideographically to denote objects and ideas.
The second fact was that they were polyphonous, each
character possessing more than one phonetic value.

For once the sceptics seemed to have common-
sense upon their side. How, it was asked, could a
system of writing be read the symbols of which might
be pronounced sometimes in one way, sometimes in
another? Anything could be made out of anything
upon such principles, and a method of interpretation
which ended in such a result was pronounced to be
self-condemned. Hincks, however, once more entered
the field and demonstrated that Rawlinson was right.[2]

[1] *Journal of the Royal Asiatic Society*, xiv.
[2] *A List of Assyro-Babylonian Characters* (1852) ; also the
Transactions of the Royal Irish Academy, xxii. (1855), and more
especially *The Polyphony of the Assyro-Babylonian Cuneiform
Writing* (1863).

Hincks was an Egyptologist, and consequently the polyphony of the cuneiform characters was not to him a new and startling phenomenon. It merely showed that they must once have been pictorial—as, indeed, their ideographic use also indicated—and in a picture-writing each picture could necessarily be represented by more than one word, and therefore by more than one phonetic value, when the pronunciation of the word came to be employed phonetically. The picture of a foot, for instance, would denote not only a "foot," but also such ideas as "go," "run," "walk," each of which would become one of its phonetic values with the development of the picture into a conventional syllabic sign.

Excavation was still proceeding on the site of Nineveh. Mr. Hormuzd Rassam, himself a native of Mossul and the active assistant of Layard, was sent in 1852 by the British Museum to complete the work from which Layard had now been called away by diplomatic duties.[1] In 1853 he made a discovery which proved to be of momentous importance for Assyrian decipherment, and without which, in fact, it could never have advanced very far. He discovered the library of Nineveh with its multitudes of closely-written clay tablets, many of them containing long lists of characters, dictionaries and grammars, which have served at once to verify and to extend the knowledge of the script and language that the early decipherers had obtained. Meanwhile a careful survey of the whole country was made at the expense of the

---

[1] See his *Asshur and the Land of Nimrod* (1898).

East India Company,[1] and the French Government sent out an exploring and excavating expedition to Babylonia under a young and brilliant scholar, Jules Oppert. The results of the mission, which lasted from 1851 to 1854, were embodied in two learned volumes, the first of which appeared in 1863.[2] In these Oppert showed, what Hincks and Rawlinson had already pointed out, that the peculiarities of the Assyrian syllabary were due not only to its pictorial origin but also to the fact that it had been invented by a non-Semitic people. This primitive population of Babylonia, called Akkadian by Hincks, Sumerian by Oppert, had spoken an agglutinative language similar to that of the Turks or Finns, and had been the founders of Babylonian civilization. For these views Oppert found support in the tablets of the library of Nineveh, a large part of which consists of translations from the older language into Semitic Assyrian, as well as of comparative grammars, vocabularies and reading-books in the two languages.

Once more the Semitic scholars protested. There was no end to the extravagant fantasies of the Assyriologists! The learned world was comfortably convinced that none but a Semitic or Aryan people could have been the originators of civilization, and to assert that the Semites had borrowed their culture from a race which seemed to have affinities with Mongols or Tatars was an outrage upon established prejudices. The Semitic philologist was more certain

---

[1] F. Jones, *Vestiges of Assyria* (1855) ; *Journal of the Royal Asiatic Society*, xv. pp. 297 *sqq.* ; and more especially *Memoirs*, edited by R. H. Thomas, 1857.
[2] *Expédition scientifique en Mésopotamie.*

than ever that Assyrian decipherment was the folly
of a few "untrained" amateurs, and could safely be
disregarded.

But the little band of Assyriologists pursued their
labours undisturbed. In 1855–6 Hincks published
a most remarkable series of articles in the *Journal
of Sacred Literature*, in which the various forms of the
Assyrian verb were analyzed and given once for all.
The work has never had to be repeated, and the
foundations of Assyrian grammar were solidly laid.
A few years later (in 1860) a complete grammar of
the language was published by Oppert. The initial
stage of Assyrian decipherment was thus at an end.

We must now turn back to the second transcript
of the Persian inscriptions, which, thanks to its greater
simplicity, had been deciphered before the Assyro-
Babylonian. The way was opened in 1844 by the
Danish scholar Westergaard.[1] With the help of the
proper names he fixed the values of many of the
characters and made a tentative endeavour to read
the texts. But the language he brought to light was
of so strange a nature as to throw doubt on the
correctness of his method. Turkish, Arabic, Indian
and even Keltic elements seemed alike to be mingled
in it. It was not, therefore, till his readings had been
subjected to revision by Hincks in 1846[2] and de Saulcy
in 1850[3] that any confidence was reposed in it, and
the results made available for the decipherment of

---

[1] In the *Zeitschrift für die Kunde des Morgenlandes*, vi.
pp. 337 *sqq.*
[2] *Transactions of the Royal Irish Academy*, xxi. pp. 114 *sqq.*
and 233 *sqq.*
[3] *Journal asiatique*, xiv. pp. 93 *sqq.* ; xv. pp. 398 *sqq.*

the Babylonian transcripts, the characters of which frequently had the same forms. It must be remembered, however, that Westergaard worked from defective materials. Rawlinson had not yet published his copy of the Behistun inscription, which he eventually placed in the hands of Edwin Norris, who, in 1853, edited the text along with a syllabary, grammar and vocabulary, as well as translations and commentary.[1] This edition was a splendid piece of work, and with it the decipherment of the second transcript of the Persian inscriptions may be said to have been accomplished. Oppert's *Peuple et Langage des Mèdes*, which appeared in 1879, did but revise, supplement and systematize the work of Norris.

The new language which had thus been brought to light was agglutinative. Westergaard had seen in it the language of the Medes, and, like Rawlinson, had connected it with a hypothetical "Scythian" family of speech. The term "Scythian" was retained by Norris, who, however, attempted to show that it was really related to the Finnish dialects. But the excavations made at Susa by Loftus in 1851 put another face on the matter. In 1874, and again more fully in 1883,[2] I pointed out that the inscriptions found at Susa and other ancient Elamite sites were in an older form of the same language as that of the second Achæmenian transcripts, and furthermore that certain inscriptions discovered by Layard in the

[1] *Journal of the Royal Asiatic Society*, xv.
[2] *Transactions of the Society of Biblical Archæology*, iii. pp 465 *sqq.*; *Actes du VIième Congrès International des Orientalistes en* 1883, ii. pp. 637 *sqq.* (1885).

plain of Mal-Amîr eastward of Susa were in practically the same script and dialect.   At the same time
I fixed the values of the characters in the Mal-Amîr
texts and gave provisional translations of them, with
a vocabulary and commentary.   Oppert and myself
had already been working at the reading of the older
Susian inscriptions, a task in which we were followed
by Weissbach with a greater measure of success.
But the same cause which had retarded the decipherment of the second transcript of the Persian inscriptions—a want of materials—militated against any
great advance being made in the decipherment of the
older Susian, and it is only since 1897, when the
excavations of M. de Morgan at Susa were begun,
that the student has been at last provided with the
necessary means.   Thanks to the brilliant penetration
of the French Assyriologist, Dr. Scheil, the outlines
of the language of the ancient kingdom of Elam
can now be sketched with a fair amount of completeness and accuracy.[1]   The name of Neo-Susian has
by common consent been conferred upon the language
of the second Achæmenian transcripts ; perhaps
Neo-Elamite would be better.   At all events it
represents the language of the second capital of the
Persian Empire as it was spoken in the age of Darius
and his successors, and is a lineal descendant of the
old agglutinative language of Elam.

The three systems of cuneiform script, which a
hundred years ago seemed so impenetrable in their
mystery, have thus, one by one, been forced to

---

[1] *Mémoires de la Délégation en Perse;* the volumes by Dr.
Scheil on the inscriptions that have thus far appeared are ii.,
iii., iv., v. and vi.

yield their secrets. But as each in turn has been deciphered, fresh forms of cuneiform writing and new languages expressed in cuneiform characters have come to light. The first to emerge was that agglutinative language of primitive Chaldæa which so scandalized the philological world and excited such strong distrust of the Assyriologists. The question of the name by which it should be called has been set at rest by the discovery of tablets in which its native designation is made known to us. Some years ago Bezold published a bilingual text in which it is termed "the language of Sumer,"[1] and more recently Messerschmidt has edited a bilingual inscription of the Babylonian king Samsu-ditana in which the Semitic "translation" is described as "Akkadian."[2] Oppert is thus shown to have been right in the name which he proposed to give to the language of the inventors of the cuneiform script.

The first analysis of Sumerian grammar was made by myself in 1870, when the general outlines of the language were fixed and the verbal forms read and explained.[3] Three years later Lenormant threw the materials I had collected into a connected and systematic form, one result of which was a controversy started by the Orientalist, Joseph Halévy, who maintained that Sumerian was not a language at all, but a cryptograph or secret writing. The answers made by the Assyriologists to this curious theory obliged its author constantly to shift his ground, but

[1] *Zeitschrift für Assyriologie*, 1889, p. 434.
[2] *Ak-ka-du; Orientalische Literatur-Zeitung*, 1905, p. 268.
[3] *Journal of Philology*, iii. pp. 1 *sqq.* I endeavoured to settle the nature of Sumerian phonology in a Memoir on "Accadian Phonology," published by the Philological Society, 1877–8.

at the same time it also obliged them to examine their materials more carefully and to revise conclusions which had been arrived at on insufficient evidence. An important discovery was now made by Haupt, who had already given the first scientific translation of a Sumerian text ;[1] he demonstrated the existence of two dialects, one of which is marked by all the phenomena of phonetic decay.[2] This was naturally supposed to indicate a difference of age in the two dialects, the one being the older and the other the later form of the language. Subsequent research, however, has gone to show that the two dialects were really used contemporaneously, the decayed state of that which was called "the woman's language" by the Babylonians being due to the fact that it was spoken in Akkad or Northern Babylonia, where the Semitic element became predominant at a much earlier period than in Sumer or Southern Babylonia.

Up to this time the study of Sumerian had been almost entirely confined to the bilingual texts, of which a very large number existed in the library of Nineveh, and in which a Semitic translation was attached to the Sumerian original. Now, however, the French excavations at Tello in Southern Babylonia began to furnish European scholars with monuments of the pre-Semitic period, and to these the decipherers, among whom Amiaud and Thureau Dangin hold the first place, accordingly turned their attention. Texts composed in days when Sumerian

---

[1] *Die Sumerischen Familiengesetze* (1879).
[2] Göttingen *Nachrichten*, 17 (1880) ; *Die Akkadische Sprache* (1883).

princes still governed the country, and written by
scribes who were unacquainted with a Semitic
language, were successfully attacked with the assistance of the bilingual tablets of Nineveh. But it was
soon found that between these genuine examples of
Sumerian composition and the Sumerian which was
written and explained by Semitic scribes there was
a good deal of difference. The Semites had derived
their culture from their Sumerian predecessors, and
a considerable part of the religious and legal literature that had been handed on to them was in the
older language. This older language long continued
to be that of both religion and law, the two conservative forces in society, Sumerian becoming to the
Semitic Babylonians what Latin was to mediæval
Europe. The inevitable result followed : Semitic
idioms and modes of thought were clothed in a
Sumerian dress, and the ignorance of the scribe
produced not infrequently the equivalent of the
dog-Latin of a modern school-boy. The gradual
changes that took place in the cuneiform system of
writing, and the adaptation of it to the requirements
of Semitic speech, contributed to the creation of an
artificial and quite unclassical Sumerian, and the
lexical tablets became filled with uses and combina-
tions of characters which were professedly Sumerian
but really Semitic in origin. All this renders the
decipherment of a Sumerian text even now a
difficult affair, and many years must elapse before
we can say that the stage of decipherment is definitely passed and that the scholar may content himself
with a purely philological treatment of the language.
But Sumerian was not the only new language

outside the circle recognized by the Persian monarchs which the decipherment of the cuneiform characters has revealed to us. Even before the discovery of Sumerian, cuneiform inscriptions had been copied on the rocks and quarried stones of Armenia, which, when the characters composing them came to be read, proved to belong to a language as novel and as apparently unrelated to any other as Sumerian itself. As far back as 1826 a young scholar of the name of Schulz had been sent by the French Government to Van in Armenia, where, according to Armenian writers, Semiramis, the fabled queen of Assyria, had once left her monuments. Here Schulz actually found that the cliff on which the ancient fortress of the city stood was covered with lines of cuneiform characters, and similar inscriptions soon came to light in other parts of the country. Before Schulz, however, could return to Europe he was murdered (in 1829) by a Kurdish chief, whose guest he had been. But his papers were recovered, and the copies of the inscriptions he had made were published in 1840 in the *Journal Asiatique*. The first to attempt to read them was Dr. Hincks, whom no problem in decipherment ever seemed to baffle.[1] The characters, he showed, were practically identical with those found in the Assyrian texts, the values of many of which had now been ascertained; but Hincks, with his usual acuteness, went on to use the Armenian or Vannic inscriptions for settling the values of other Assyrian characters which had not as yet been determined. In 1848 he was already able to read the names of the Vannic kings and fix

[1] *Journal of the Royal Asiatic Society*, 1848, ix. pp. 387 *sqq.*

their succession, to make out the sense of several passages in the texts, and to indicate the nominative and accusative suffixes of the noun.

Here Vannic decipherment rested for many years. There was no difficulty in reading the inscriptions phonetically, for they were written in a very simplified form of the Assyrian syllabary; but the language which was thus revealed stood isolated and alone, without linguistic kindred either ancient or modern. The various attempts made to decipher it were all failures.

So things remained until 1882–3, when I published my Memoir on "The Decipherment of the Vannic Inscriptions" in the *Journal of the Royal Asiatic Society*. Here for the first time translations were given of the inscriptions, together with a commentary, grammar and vocabulary. At the same time I settled the chronological place of the Vannic kings, which had hitherto been uncertain, as well as the geography of the country over which they ruled, and analyzed the ancient religion of the people as made known to us by the decipherment of the texts. In revising and supplementing Schulz's copies of the inscriptions I had obtained the help of squeezes taken by Layard and Rassam. The task of decipherment was, after all, not so hard a matter as the absence of a bilingual text might make it appear. The want of a bilingual was compensated by the numerous ideographs and "determinatives" scattered through the inscriptions, which indicated their general meaning, pointed out to the decipherer the names of countries, cities, individuals and the like, and gave him the significa-tion of the phonetically-written words which in parallel passages often replaced them. Moreover, the French Assyriologist, Stanislas Guyard, and myself had independently made the discovery that a clause which frequently comes at the end of a Vannic inscription corresponds with the imprecatory formula of the Assyrians, while the decipherment of the inscriptions led to the further discovery that not only had the characters employed in them been borrowed from the Assyrians in the time of the Assyrian conqueror, Assur-natsir-pal, but that many of the phrases used in Assur-natsir-pal's texts had been borrowed at the same time.

Other scholars soon appeared to pursue and extend my work, more especially Drs. Beick and Lehmann, whose expedition to Armenia in 1898 has placed at our disposal a large store of fresh material. Amongst this fresh material are two long bilingual inscriptions, in Vannic and Assyrian, one of which had been discovered by de Morgan in 1890. These have verified my system of decipherment, have increased our knowledge of the Vannic vocabulary, have corrected a few errors, and, I am bound to add, have in one or two cases justified renderings of mine to which exception had been taken. A historical Vannic text can now be read with almost as much certainty as an Assyrian one.

With the discovery of the language spoken in Armenia before the arrival of the modern Armenians the list of lost languages and dialects brought to light by the decipherment of the cuneiform script is by no means exhausted. Among the tablets found in 1887 at Tel el-Amarna in Upper Egypt was a long letter from the king of Mitanni or Northern Mesopotamia in the native language of his country,

C

which has been partially deciphered by Messer-schmidt, Jensen and myself.[1] The language turns out to be distantly related to the Vannic, but is of a much more complicated description. Two of the other letters in the same collection were in yet another previously unknown language, which the contents of one of them showed to be that of a kingdom in Asia Minor called Arzawa. Since then tablets have been found at Boghaz Keui in Cappadocia, on the site of the ancient capital of the Hittites, which are in the same dialect and form of cuneiform writing, and prove that in them we have discovered at last actual relics of the Hittite tongue. Thanks to the light thrown upon them by a tablet from the same locality, which I obtained last year, it is now possible to raise the veil which has hitherto concealed the Hittite language, and in a Paper which will shortly be printed I have succeeded in partially translating the texts and sketching the outlines of their grammar. But any detailed account of these discoveries must be reserved for a future chapter; at present I can do no more than refer briefly to these latest problems in cuneiform decipherment.

That other problems still await us cannot be doubted. The number of different languages which the decipherment of the cuneiform script has thus far revealed to us is an assurance that, as excavation and research proceed, fresh languages will come to light which have employed the cuneiform syllabary as a

---

[1] See my article, "On the Language of Mitanni," in the *Proceedings of the Society of Biblical Archæology*, 1900, pp. 171 *sqq.*; and Leopold Messerschmidt in the *Mitteilungen der Vorderasiatischen Gesellschaft*, 1899, part iv. pp. 175 *sqq.*

means of expression. Indeed, we already know that it was used by the Kossæans, wild mountaineers who skirted the eastern frontiers of Babylonia, and a list of whose words has been preserved in a cuneiform tablet,[1] and also that there was a time, before the introduction of the Phœnician alphabet, when "the language of Canaan"—better known as Hebrew—was written in cuneiform characters. Canaanite glosses are found in the Tel el-Amarna tablets, and two Sidonian seals exist in which the cuneiform syllabary is employed to represent the sounds of Canaanitish speech.[2]

And the key to all this varied literature, this medley of languages, the very names of which had perished, was a simple guess! But it was a scientific guess, made in accordance with scientific method, and based upon sound scientific reasoning. It is true that it needed the slow and patient work of generations of scholars before the guess could ripen into maturity; the discovery of the value of a single letter in the Old Persian alphabet was sometimes the labour of a lifetime; but, like the seed of the mustard tree, the guess contained within itself all the promise of its future growth. On the day when Grotefend identified the names of Darius and Xerxes, the decipherment of the cuneiform inscriptions, and therewith of the history, the theology and the civilization of the ancient Oriental world, was potentially accomplished.

[1] Fr. Delitzsch, *Die Sprache der Kossäer* (1884).
[2] They are now in the possession of M. de Clercq. For a translation of the inscriptions upon them, see my *Patriarchal Palestine*, p. 250.

CHAPTER II

THE modern science ot archæology has been
derisively called "the study of pots." As a matter of
fact, the study of ancient pottery occupies a prominent
place in it, and we cannot turn over the pages of
a standard archæological work without constantly
coming across photographs and illustrations of the
ceramic art or reading descriptions of vases and
bowls, of coloured ware and fragmentary sherds.
Questions of date and origin are made to turn on the
presence or absence of some particular form of pottery
on a given site, and fierce controversies have arisen
over a single fragment of a vessel of clay. A knowledge of ancient pottery is a primary requisite in the
scientific excavator and archæologist of to-day.

The reason of this is obvious. Archæology is an
inductive science ; its conclusions, therefore, are drawn
from the comparison and co-ordination of objects
which can be seen and handled, as well as tested by
all competent observers. It is built upon what our
German friends would call objective facts, and the
method it employs is that carefully-disciplined and
experimentally-guarded application of the ordinary
logic of life which can alone give us scientific results.

The method is one which the purely literary mind seems often curiously incapable of comprehending; the literary student is accustomed to deal so exclusively with matters of merely individual taste and theory that he is as little able to understand what is meant by scientific evidence and probability as the scholar who is not a mathematician is able to follow the reasoning of Lord Kelvin. This is a fact which has to be borne in mind more especially in archæological science, for the questions with which archæology is concerned so frequently invade the domain of literature or appear so closely connected with questions that are more or less literary, that the purely literary scholar is apt to think himself just as well qualified to discuss them as "the man in the street" is apt to think himself qualified to discuss the etymology of a word. To all such the archæologist would say, "Go and study your pots."

For pottery is practically indestructible. Like the fossils on which the geologist has built up the past history of life upon the earth, it is an enduring evidence, when rightly interpreted, of the past history of man. Like the fossils, moreover, it exhibits a multitudinous variety of types and forms. But in all these types and forms there is an underlying unity. The primitive needs of man are everywhere the same, and the powers of mind called in to supply them are the same also. The dish and bowl, the vase and its handles, meet us again and again wherever we go; and the same materials for making them meet us also. The hands of man, guided by the brain of man, found clay wherewith to manufacture the vessels that he needed, and to harden it afterwards in the sun or fire.

Where or how the first pottery was made we do not know, we probably shall never know. When palæolithic man first makes his appearance in Europe he seems not yet to have been acquainted with it ; but it is difficult to prove a negative in archæology as in other sciences, and the absence of palæolithic pottery may be due only to the imperfection of the record. At any rate, as we descend the ladder of chronology the existence of man is marked more and more by the fragments of pottery he has left behind him; at Rome a whole mountain of it grew up in the space of a few centuries, and the huge mounds that encircled Cairo a hundred years ago were mainly formed of mediæval sherds. When excavating on an Egyptian site I have sometimes been tempted to think that the people who once lived there must have spent their whole time in breaking their household ware.

Now not only are the primitive needs of man much the same throughout the world and at all periods of time, the nature of man is much the same also ; and a distinguishing feature in his nature is love of variety. The same variety which we see in the forms of life and in the outward appearance and mental aptitudes of man himself is reflected in the products of his skill. Yet along with this love of variety goes a strong conservative or imitative instinct—an instinct which finds, too, its counterpart in nature, " so careful of the type." On the one hand, fashions change ; on the other, a fashion once introduced spreads rapidly and maintains itself to the exclusion of all others for a determinate period of time throughout a determinate area. And to nothing does this apply with more truth than to pottery. Observation has shown that not only are different tribes or countries distinguished by a difference in their pottery, but that in each tribe or country similar differences distinguish successive periods of time. When to this is added the practical indestructibility of the potsherd, it will easily be seen what a criterion is afforded by it for fixing the age and character of ancient remains, and their relation to other monuments of the past. It is not surprising that a study of pottery has become the sheet-anchor of archæological chronology, and that the first object of the scientific excavator is to determine the relative succession of the ceramic remains he discovers and their connection with similar remains found elsewhere. Scientific excavation means, before all things else, careful observation and record of every piece of pottery, however apparently worthless, which the excavator disinters.

But now, unfortunately, I have to make an admission. We have, as yet, no ceramic record in either Babylonia or Assyria. Until very recently there has been no attempt in either country at scientific excavation. The pioneers, Layard and Botta and Loftus, lived and worked before it was known or thought of, and we cannot, therefore, be too thankful to Layard for having nevertheless given us so full and accurate an account of what he found, and the conditions under which he found it. The excavations controlled by the British Museum have, I am sorry to say, been for the most part destructive rather than scientific; such objects as were wanted by the Museum were alone sought after; little or no record has been kept of their discovery, and they have been mixed with objects bought from natives, of whose origin nothing was

known. At one spot, Carchemish, the old Hittite
capital, which, though not strictly in Assyria, formed
part of the Assyrian Empire, and was the seat of an
Assyrian governor, the so-called excavations conducted by the Museum in 1880 were simply a scandal,
which Dr. Hayes Ward, who visited the spot shortly
afterwards, has characterized as "wicked." The
archæological evidence there, which would have
thrown so much light on the Hittite problem, has
been irretrievably lost.

Matters are better now, and if I may judge from the
work done by Mr. H. R. Hall at Dêr el-Bâharî in
Egypt for the Egypt Exploration Fund, his colleague,
Mr. L. W. King, who has recently been excavating
for the British Museum in Assyria, will have done
something to retrieve the archæological good name of
our British excavators in the East. M. de Sarzec's
excavations at Tello in Southern Babylonia were also
conducted with some consideration for archæological
method, at all events on the architectural side, and in
the capable hands of M. Heuzey the works of art found
there have been made to yield valuable results.
Moreover, the history of Tello may be said to be comprised in a single epoch of archaic Babylonia, and all
objects discovered on the site may consequently be
regarded as belonging to one age and phase of Babylonian civilization. Of the American excavations at
Niffer it is difficult to speak at present. The work
there has been careful and patient, and has extended
over a long series of years. The architectural facts
have been accurately recorded, at all events in the
case of the great temple of Bel, and about the sequence
of the inscribed monuments there is little room for

doubt. But accusations of carelessness have lately
been brought by the excavators one against the other,
and when we find the sharpest critic among them
unable to substantiate his own account of the discovery of a library and implicitly endorsing the
assignment of a Parthian palace to the " Mykenæan "
age, it is impossible to put much faith in their descriptions of archæological details. Some years ago the
Germans explored a cemetery at El-Hibba with considerable care and thoroughness, and thus revealed to
us pretty much all we know at present about Babylonian funereal customs ; yet here again too little
attention was paid to the pottery, and the actual date
of the cemetery is still uncertain. It may belong to
the Babylonian period, but it may also not be older
than the Persian or even Parthian age.

The Germans are once more working in the lands
of the Euphrates and Tigris, but in Babylonia their
labours have been mainly confined to the Babylon of
Nebuchadrezzar, where comparatively little has been
discovered. Since 1904, however, the chief strength
of the expedition has been directed upon Qal'at
Shirqât, where Assur, the primitive capital of Assyria
formerly stood, and here we may expect that archæological results of first-class importance will at last be
obtained. But the work there has not yet advanced far
enough for more to be done than the mapping out of
the old city, the ascertainment of certain architectural
facts, and the recovery of inscriptions of great historical
value.

It will be seen, therefore, that the reproach brought
against excavations in Egypt by Mr. Rhind in 1862
still holds good of excavations in Babylonia and

Assyria. The first stage in their history is only just passing away. The idea that excavation is a trade which any one can take up without previous training, and that all the excavator need think about is the discovery of objects for a museum, is only beginning to disappear. In 1862 Rhind could write of Egyptian tombs: "I am not aware that there can be found the contents of a single sepulchre duly authenticated with satisfactory precision as to what objects were present, and as to the relative positions all these occupied when deposited by contemporary hands. Indeed, for many of the Egyptian sepulchral antiquities scattered over Europe there exists no record to determine even the part of the country where they were exhumed. . . . There have thus been swept away unrecorded into the past illustrative facts of very great interest, which cannot now, according to any reasonable probability, be replaced, at all events in the degree which there are grounds to believe were then possible." [1] Happily, Mr. Rhind's words are no longer true of Egypt, where he himself set the first example of showing how scientific exploration ought to be carried on, and the result is that the ancient civilization and culture of Egypt are now known to us even better than those of classical Greece or Rome.

But what was true in 1862 of Egypt is still very largely true of Assyria and Babylonia. We are beginning to know something about the history of Assyro-Babylonian architecture ; we know a little about the early work of the Babylonians in metal and stone ; but the history of Assyro-Babylonian pottery is still, speaking broadly, a blank. For most of his know-

[1] *Thebes, its Tombs and their Tenants*, pp. 62, 66.

ledge of the ancient Euphratean civilizations the
archæologist has to turn to the inscriptions and
written literature of which such vast quantities have
survived, and hence, besides being an archæologist in
the strict sense, he must be also a decipherer and a
philologist. He is still precluded from appealing to
the evidence which can be handled and felt.

From the point of view of the archæologist written
evidence is usually unsatisfactory because it admits
of more than one interpretation. A translation
which seems certain to one scholar may be questioned
by another; an inference drawn from the words of
a text by one student may be denied by another.
The statements in the texts themselves may be
contradictory, or their imperfection may lead to
wrong conclusions. Above all, the evidence may
come to the archæologist from a philologist whose
bent of mind is literary rather than scientific, and who
will therefore be unable either to appreciate or to
understand scientific testimony. Nothing is more
common than to come across literary critics who
cannot be made to understand the nature of inductive
proof.

On the other hand, the decipherer of a lost language
must necessarily be an archæologist as well. The
clues he follows will be largely archæological, and
he has to appeal to archæology at every step. The
method he must pursue is the method of archæology
and of other inductive sciences, and the materials he
uses are in part the materials of archæology also.
The philologist who knows nothing of history and
geography, who is unable to follow a scientific argument and appreciate scientific reasoning, can never

decipher ; he may take the materials given him by the decipherer and work them into philological shape, but that is all. We must listen to him on questions of grammar and vocabulary ; on questions of archæology his opinions are worth no more than those of the ordinary man.

I have insisted on this point because it is a very important one in a study like Assyriology. The public naturally thinks that in all Assyriological matters the opinion of one Assyriologist is as good as that of another. We might just as well suppose that in all matters which come under the head of astronomy the opinions of every class of astronomer are equally authoritative. But in astronomy there are questions which are purely mathematical, and there are other questions which are more or less chemical, and the astronomer who has devoted his attention to the spectrum analysis is contented to leave to his mathematical colleague abstruse calculations in advanced mathematics. The Assyriologist who is a grammarian pure and simple is just as little an authority on the archæological side of his study as any one else who is ignorant of archæology, and the materials he provides must be dealt with by the archæologist like the literary materials provided for him by the classical philologist ; the materials in both cases stand on the same footing.

At the same time, there is a difference between them. In the first place, the literary materials with which the Assyriologist deals are in a very large number of instances autographs. They are the actual documents of the writers whose names they bear or to whose age they belong. And there is all

the difference in the world between the letters of
a Plato or a Cicero which have come down to
us through numerous copyists and the letters of
Khammu-rabi of Babylon, the originals of which
are now in our hands. The inscriptions in which
Nebuchadrezzar describes his building operations or
the contemporaneous annals of the Assyrian kings
are, from the historical point of view, of far more
value than the books written about them at a later date,
however admirable the latter may be as works of
literature ; in other words, they are first-hand sources,
and, as such, objective facts of much the same
character as ancient pottery or stone implements.
Then, in the second place, the documents have to be
deciphered before they can be treated philologically ;
and, as I have already said, the task of decipherment
is in itself an archæological pursuit. If carried out
on correct lines it is itself an instance of the application of the inductive method, and it is, moreover,
constantly compelled to call archæology or history
to its aid. Assyriology is thus primarily an archæological study, using the methods of archæological
science and demanding the help of the archæologist,
even though there are Assyriologists who are not
archæologists themselves.

But for the present our archæological facts have
to be taken mainly from the results of the decipherment of the inscriptions. They are for the most
part epigraphical ; the excavator has not yet supplemented them, as in Egypt or prehistoric Greece,
on what I would term the ceramic side. This,
at least, is the case in Babylonia and Assyria. It
is no longer the case, however, throughout the ancient

Assyro-Babylonian world. There is one exception to the charge brought by modern archæology against the excavators in the lands of the Tigris and Euphrates. M. de Morgan has been working for the last ten years on the site of Susa, the capital of Elam, and he has brought to his labours the knowledge and experience of an excavator who has been trained in modern methods and is fully awake to the requirements of modern science. At last, at Susa, we have an archæological record of the history of culture, based not only on written monuments, but also on the more tangible evidence of scientifically-observed strata of human remains. It is true that Elam is not Babylonia ; but one of the surprises of M. de Morgan's discoveries is that in the early days of Babylonian history Elam was a Babylonian province, and Susa the seat of a Babylonian governor. The same culture extended from Sippara on the Euphrates to Susa in Elam, and this culture was Babylonian. Hence, in default of materials from Babylonia itself, we may see in the history of cultural development at Susa a counterpart of that in Babylonia, at any rate during the period when Elam and Babylonia were alike under Semitic rule.[1]

At Susa the line of division between the prehistoric or neolithic age and the historical epoch is very clearly marked. The prehistoric stratum lies twenty-five metres below the surface of the mounds, and is divided by M. de Morgan and his fellow-workers into

---

[1] For the archæological results of M. de Morgan's work, see his *Mémoires de la Délégation en Perse*, vols. i. and vii. The eighth volume, which will also be devoted to archæology, is in preparation.

two periods. The first is distinguished by a fine thin pottery, with yellow paste, which is already made upon a wheel. It does not exceed from two to seven millimetres in thickness ; it is polished, and decorated with black bands and various patterns in a brown colour produced by oxide of iron. The designs are not only geometric, but also represent animal and vegetable forms. Among them are rows of ostriches identical with those found on the painted prehistoric pottery of Egypt. Indeed, the explorers were especially struck by the resemblance of the pottery as a whole to that of Egypt in the prehistoric age, though it is difficult to see what connection there can have been between the two countries at so remote a date, and the curious similarity between the rows of birds depicted on the vases must remain for the present an archæological puzzle. There is also a certain amount of resemblance between the geometric pottery and that disinterred by M. Chantre at the early Assyrian colony at Kara Eyuk in Cappadocia, which will be discussed more fully in a later chapter.[1] Among the geometrical patterns of the Susian ware spherical forms are common ; the herring-bone pattern is also met with, as well as a pattern like the Greek *sigma*. The under-part of the vases is often decorated, so also is the inside. A form of vase frequently found is the water-jar with a rounded foot ; the goblet is another common shape. Sometimes the vases are supplied with four handles for suspension.

This fine yellow pottery occurs not only at Susa, but also throughout Elam, but practically none of it

[1] Chantre, *Mission en Cappadoce*, plates x.–xii.

has hitherto been discovered in Babylonia.[1]   One cause of this is doubtless that in the alluvial plain of Babylonia a purely neolithic stratum, if it existed at all, would lie below the water-level. Maritime shells are met with as far north as the site of Babylon, showing that the Persian Gulf once extended thus far, and the water of the Euphrates still infiltrates through the soil.

The period of the fine thin pottery in Elam comes suddenly to an end, and the people of the second prehistoric period seem to have been intruders who were less civilized than their predecessors and un-acquainted with the art of making the older ware. Their pottery is coarse and porous, and the geometric designs upon it are traced with the pen, not freely painted as in the case of the earlier ceramic. The animal and vegetable designs of the older ware have disappeared, and the zones, triangles and other geometric figures which take their place are traced in black or maroon-red upon a yellow clay. The resemblance between this pottery and that of Kara Eyuk is even greater than in the case of the pottery of the first period. Thick cylindrical vases are com-mon, as well as bowls with a flat bottom and broad sides. Some of the vases resemble the bulbous vases of the Egyptian Twelfth dynasty ; there are others

---

[1] The yellow and red wheel-made ware, some of it inscribed with characters of the age of Gudea, which has been disinterred at Tello, is quite different. This class of pottery, by the way, seems to have been preceded by a grey coarse ware, made with the hand. One fragment of fine polished yellow ware with traces of black ornamentation has recently been reported from Tello by Captain Cros (*Revue d'Assyriologie*, 1905, p. 59), but the isolated character of the discovery makes it probable that it was an importation from Elam.

with flat bottoms and angular sides which are also like Egyptian water-jars of the same Twelfth-dynasty period. Along with these more characteristic forms of pottery many small, unpainted cups have been found, as well as a few finer wheel-made vases of ovoid shape and yellow or reddish colour. It should be added that coarse, red, hand-made pottery abounds in both the prehistoric periods, as indeed it does also in the later historic epoch.

As the second prehistoric epoch drew to a close at Susa, many indications of an advance in culture began to show themselves. Vases and flat-bottomed cups of soft stone were introduced, among them being a few of alabaster ; the bricks began to be burnt in a kiln, and even seals with a species of writing upon them made their appearance. Nevertheless, the neolithic age does not pass into the age of metal through any transitional stages.

The earliest stratum which marks the historic age yields for the first time clay tablets with inscriptions, the characters of which are already developing out of pictures into the cursive cuneiform. The inscribed cylinder-seals of Babylonia naturally appear along with them ; alabaster vases, cups and bowls become common, and some of them are cut into the forms of animals. Comparatively little pottery has been found in this stratum ; but this is probably an accident.

The next stratum brings us to the period of Babylonian supremacy, when the viceroys of the Babylonian king ruled at Susa, and Semitic influence was already predominant in the Babylonian plain. It is the age of Sargon of Akkad, and its commencement may approximately be placed about B.C. 4000.

D

The pottery still consists of a yellow paste, though there are also many specimens of a coarse black clay decorated with incrustations in white. The yellow ware is occasionally ornamented with mouldings of trees and other natural objects. A typical vase of the period is one of globular shape and small rim, and with a moulded or incised rope-pattern running round the centre and lower part of the rim. Another type is one which looks like an inverted vase, with a series of rope-patterns encircling it, while another seems to have been copied from the pile of cylindrical vases into which, as into a drain, the body of the dead Babylonian was inserted. These types of vase appear to have lasted, with little variation, down to the end of the Persian period, though, unfortunately, the disturbance of the ground and the consequent mixture of objects under the temple of In-Susinak, where the excavations were carried on, makes certainty on the point unattainable. Immense quantities of bronze votive offerings, of all kinds and sorts, were, however, found here, along with fragments of glass, and, as inscriptions show that they must all have been buried on the spot before the tenth century B.C., we have a time-limit for dating the forms of the bronze weapons and tools.

The archæological evidence obtained at Susa has been supplemented by excavations made some ninety miles to the west of it, at a place called Mussian, on the eastern bank of the river Tib. Here there are graves, as well as the remains of a temple and houses with vaults, columns and walls of burnt brick. Where the strata have allowed a section to be cut down to the virgin soil the results are found to agree with those revealed by the excavations at Susa. The earliest layer belongs to the neolithic age, flint and obsidian, as at Susa, being the materials employed for tools and weapons. The pottery is thick and hand-made, the paste being either yellow or red in colour, and the surface is often polished, while many of the vases are furnished with holes for suspension. This layer seems older than anything discovered at Susa. It is followed by a second layer, in which the pottery is wheel-made, and is decorated with animal and vegetable figures in black or red, like the first prehistoric ware of the Susa mounds. Among the animal figures are those of men, and one fragment of yellow ware is ornamented with the so-called swastika. In the upper part of the layer a few fragments of copper have been met with, indicating that the neolithic age was beginning to pass into that of copper.

Above this layer is a third, characterized by a fine ware, usually yellow but sometimes greenish in colour, and decorated with designs in lustrous black. In the fine specimens the decoration has been laid on before firing, in other cases after firing. The pottery as a whole has a general resemblance to that of prehistoric Egypt. The culture represented by this layer was still neolithic, but objects of copper were making their appearance, and the flint instruments of the past were beginning to be superseded by metal, a knowledge of which appears to have come from abroad. With the introduction of copper the Elamite or historical epoch may be said to have begun. It was now that the temple was first built of crude bricks, reeds taking the place of wood, and so pointing to the influence of

Babylonia, where reeds were plentiful and wood was scarce.

Another proof of Babylonian influence must be seen not only in ware of Babylonian origin, but also in the figures of a nude goddess with the hands placed upon the breasts, which originally represented the divinity called Istar by the Semitic Babylonians. Indeed, from the fact that the goddess was represented in human form we may infer that the figures, though first met with in the Sumerian age, were of Semitic derivation, and show that Sumerian culture was already being affected by the influence of Semitic religious ideas.[1] The pottery found along with the figures is of a very varied description, including coarse red and fine yellow ware. Among the fine yellow ware are goblets with a tall cup supported on a foot. A typical form of the yellow ware is the vase with angular sides ; this, together with vases of more bulbous shape and terra-cotta stands, is remarkably like some of the Egyptian Twelfth-dynasty pottery in form. The stands, more especially, remind us of Twelfth-dynasty Egypt. There is also a black ware decorated with incised lines which are filled in with white. This black ware is also found in Egypt, where Professor Petrie is now inclined to associate it with the Hyksos. At all events it is absent there during the interval that elapsed between the prehistoric period and the epoch of the Twelfth dynasty, and it characterizes the Hyksos sites of the Delta, while its

---

[1] Copper figurines of the goddess, with hands pressed under the breasts, found in one of the earliest substructures of Tello (*circa* B.C. 4000), are published by M. Heuzey in the *Revue d'Assyriologie*, 1899, p. 44.

foreign and non-Egyptian character has been recognized from the first. A few fragments of the same class of pottery have been brought to light at Tello in Babylonia, where they would appear to belong to the age of Gudea (B.C. 2700). One of these formed part of a cylindrical vase or pyxis, identical in shape with the black incised pyxides found at Susa at a depth of from five to ten metres below the surface. On another fragment are spirited drawings of a water-bird, a fish seized by a gull, a four-footed animal, and a boat with reeds growing behind it, each in a separate panel.[1] Similar ware has been discovered in Southern Palestine, on the eastern coast of Cyprus, in Spain and in the Greek islands. At Syros, for instance, where it goes back to the neolithic age, it is associated with alabaster vases, just as it is at Mussian. Here the bowls and vases of alabaster are strikingly Egyptian in form.

The clay figures of the Babylonian goddess testify to the same extension of culture in the copper age of Western Asia as do the black incised vases with their white fillings. M. Chantre has found them at Kara Eyuk in Cappadocia, on the borders of the Hittite region, though in these the arms are no longer folded across the breast. Further west I have lately shown [2]

---

[1] Heuzey, in the *Revue d'Assyriologie*, 1905, pp. 59 *sqq.* and plate iii. Von Lichtenberg (*Mitteilungen der Vorderasiatischen Gesellschaft*, 1906, 2) has lately pointed out that the black incised pottery with white fillings is identical in Cyprus, Troy, the Laibach bog and the Mondsee, and that the ornamentation which characterizes it is found in the valley of the Danube and the pile-dwellings of Switzerland. His attempt to derive it from Cyprus, however, cannot be sustained in view of its occurrence in Elam.

[2] *Proceedings of the Society of Biblical Archæology*, 1905, p. 28.

that the so-called figure of Niobê on Mount Sipylus in Lydia is a Hittite modification of them, and Dr. Schliemann discovered one of them, of lead, in the ruins of the Second (prehistoric) city at Troy.[1] At Troy, however, the type was more usually modified in the Hittite direction, as it was also in the islands of the Ægean, where marble figures of the goddess are plentiful.[2] In Egypt clay figures closely resembling those of Babylonia and Elam, but with the arms outstretched, have been met with from time to time at Karnak, and supposed to be dolls of the Roman period ; but since the discovery by M. Legrain of remains which prove that the history of Karnak reaches back to the prehistoric or early dynastic period, there is no longer any reason for not connecting them with their analogues elsewhere. And the discoveries recently made by Professor Pumpelly in the tumuli near Askabad, west of Khiva and Herat, go far towards supporting the identification. Here the explorers have brought to light two periods of neolithic culture, in the earlier of which no animals were as yet domesticated, and the pottery was of the rudest description. During the second period the domesticated animals were introduced, including the horse and camel. Then came an age of copper, accompanied by figurines representing the Babylonian

---

[1] *Ilios*, p. 337. Schliemann called it the Third city. Dörpfeld's subsequent excavations, however, have shown that it really was the Second city, whose history fell into three periods.

[2] Some of these represent the goddess with the arms folded, and not pressed against the breasts. See, for example, the photograph of one found at Naxos in the *Comptes rendus du Congrès international d Archéologie*, 1905, p. 221. For Trojan examples, see *Ilios*, pp. 331–6.

goddess, sometimes with the arms outstretched, sometimes with them lying against the sides, as in Cappadocia. The figurines are evidence that the art of working copper was derived from Babylonia, a conclusion which is confirmed by M. Henri de Morgan's excavations in the tumuli of Talîsh in Gîlân, on the south-western shore of the Caspian.[1] As far back as our knowledge of Babylonian history extends the inhabitants of the country were acquainted with copper, and its use lasted century after century into quite recent times. Of a stone age, as I have already said, there is no clear trace. It is true that Captain Cros has sunk shafts at Tello, and reached the virgin soil at a depth of seventeen metres, finding there mace-heads of alabaster and hard stone similar to those of primitive Egypt, as well as other stone objects; but no flint flakes were met with, and the pottery was similar to that of the higher strata.[2] On the other hand, objects of copper, great and small, including helmets and a colossal spear dedicated by a king of Kis, have been disinterred, though nothing of bronze has been discovered among the earlier remains. It was the same at Muqayyar, the ancient Ur, as well as on the site of Eridu, where Taylor found only copper bowls and the like in the graves, even in those of so late a date as to contain objects

---

[1] See *Mémoires de la Délégation en Perse*, viii. pp. 336–7. A report of some of the results of the Pumpelly expedition is given by Dr. Hubert Schmidt in the *Zeitschrift für Ethnologie* 1906, Pt. iii. p. 385.

[2] Flint implements, however, were discovered by Taylor in his excavations at Abu Shahrein, the site of Eridu (*Journal of the Royal Asiatic Society*, xv. p. 410 and plate ii.).

of iron and an Egyptian scarab.[1]   At Niffer, moreover, the ancient Nippur, American excavation has
the same tale to tell. According to Dr. Peters,[2]
though iron knives, hatchets, spear-heads and arrow-
heads have been exhumed, the date of which is said
to be between 2000 and 1000 B.C., there is no trace
of bronze, the multitudinous objects, which further
west would have been of bronze, being here of copper.
As at Ur, the copper age lasts down to the very
end of the Babylonian kingdom.   Hilprecht, on the
authority of Haynes, does indeed say[3] that in the
very lowest strata of the temple mound, far below the
pavements of Sargon and Naram-Sin (B.C. 3750),
" fragments of copper, bronze and terra-cotta vessels "
were disinterred. But no attempt seems to have
been made to analyze the so-called "bronze," which
may have been a natural alloy of copper with a small
percentage of lead or antimony, and the age ascribed
to the fragments is rendered doubtful by the accom-
panying statement, that "fragments of red and black
lacquered pottery" were discovered in the same
place which were indistinguishable from the red and
black pottery of classical Greece. As yet, therefore,
excavation in Babylonian lands has failed to tell
us when the art of mixing tin with the copper
was discovered and copper was superseded by
bronze.

   This, however, had taken place before the com-

---

[1] See Taylor's "Notes on the Ruins of Muqeyer," in the
Journal of the Royal Asiatic Society, xv. pp. 271-3 and
415.

[2] *Nippur*, vol. ii. pp. 381-6.

[3] *The Babylonian Expedition of the University of Pennsyl-
vania*, i. 2, pp. 26-7.

mencement of the Assyrian age. The bronze scimitar of Hadad-nirari I. (B.C. 1330)[1] finds an exact copy in a scimitar discovered by Mr. Macalister at Gezer in Palestine,[2] and the tools and weapons exhumed at Nineveh are of bronze and not copper. Analysis shows that the bronze usually consisted of about one part of tin to ten of copper, though for special objects like bells the amount of tin was considerably increased.[3] When was it that the tin was first imported and intentionally mixed with the copper in order to harden the metal?

In default of archæological evidence, the only possibility there is of discovering an answer to this question lies in an examination of the primitive pictures out of which the cuneiform characters eventually developed. Here we are at once struck by a curious fact. The "determinative" attached to ideographs signifying "knife," "weapon" and the like is not an ideograph which expresses the name of a metal; nor is it an ideograph denoting "stone," but one which means "wood." That is to say, the material of which cutting instruments were made at the time when the picture-writing of Babylonia came into existence was neither metal nor stone, but wood. That it should not have been stone is explained by the geology of the Babylonian plain, which consists of alluvial soil devoid of stones. That it should not have been of metal can only mean that the inventors of the pictorial script were not yet acquainted with

---

[1] *Transactions of the Society of Biblical Archæology*, 1876, pp. 347–8.
[2] Figured in the *Quarterly Statement of the Palestine Exploration Fund*, October 1904, p. 335.
[3] Layard, *Nineveh and Babylon*, pp. 571-3.

the use of copper, bronze or iron. In default of metal and stone they had to content themselves with hard wood.

On the other hand, copper, as well as gold and silver, had become known to them when the primitive pictographs were still in process of formation, and long before they had passed into cursive cuneiform. Copper was represented by the picture of an ingot or square plate of the metal with a handle attached to it, showing that it was already in a fused and worked state when it was imported into Babylonia. Gold seems to have originally been denoted by the picture of a collar or necklace, which signified "shining," and was afterwards employed before the names of the precious metals. I have, however, never found this collar actually used to signify "gold"; in the earliest texts yet discovered the phonetic syllable *gi* is attached to it when "gold" is denoted, the Sumerian word for "gold" being *azag-gi*. "Silver" was "the white precious metal," the symbol for "white" being attached to the picture of the collar, and so forming a compound ideograph. This implies that silver became known to the inventors of the hieroglyphs at a later period than gold, though still before what I will call the cuneiform age. Even iron was known to them at the same early epoch, and was expressed by ideographs which literally mean " stone of heaven,"[1] an indication that meteoric iron must be referred to.

---

[1] ANA-BAR. *Bar* is given as the Sumerian pronunciation of the word for "stone" (*Syllabary* 5, iv. 11, in Delitzsch's *Assyrische Lesestücke*, 3rd edition). In Old Egyptian "iron" was similarly *ba-n-pet*, "stone of heaven," while "silver" was "white gold," "gold" being symbolized by a collar. We may compare

But now comes a fact which is difficult to explain, so contrary is it to the archæological evidence. As we have seen, no traces of bronze have been found in the Assyro-Babylonian region before the beginning of the Assyrian age—let us say about B.C. 2000. Nevertheless, by the side of the simple ideograph which denotes the Sumerian *urudu*, " copper "—*erû* in Semitic Babylonian—we find a compound ideograph signifying " bronze," called *zabar* in Sumerian, from which the Semites borrowed their *'siparru*. It is true that it is a compound ideograph, but it occurs in the cuneiform texts, not only in the era of Gudea (B.C. 2700), but even before the age of Sargon of Akkad (B.C. 3800). And an analysis of its earliest form seems to indicate that it really must have meant bronze from the first, and that consequently there was no transference of signification in later days. Literally it means " white copper," the word for " copper " being phonetically written *ka-mas*, with which the Semitic Babylonian *kemassu* is closely connected. Lead cannot be intended, as that was denoted by a different word and different ideographs, and I do not see what else " white copper " can be in contradistinction to red copper except bronze. Polished

---

the Indo-European "white " metal as a name of " silver." The Sumerian *azaggi*, " gold," was a form of *azagga*, " precious," more especially " precious metal " ; the more specific word for " gold " was *guskin*, with which the Armenian *oski* must be connected. " Silver " was *bábara*, the " bright " metal, *nagga* being " lead," the Armenian *anag*. The identity of the Armenian and Sumerian words for " gold " and " lead," coupled with the Armenian origin of the vine, and the fact that the mountain on which the ark of the Babylonian Noah rested was Jebel Judi, south of Lake Van, raises an interesting question as to the origin of Sumerian civilization.

copper could be termed "bright," but hardly "white."[1]

The possibility remains that tin might have been the metal originally denoted by the compound ideograph. If so, both the ideograph and the words expressed by it had lost all reference to tin before the beginning of the Assyrian period, and neither the Assyrian word for "tin" nor the Sumerian word, if any existed, is now known. Tin, moreover, was archæologically late in making its appearance. The earliest examples of pure tin of which I know are of the time of the Eighteenth Egyptian dynasty. On the other hand, bronze first appears in Egypt in the age of the Twelfth dynasty,[2] though it does not

---

[1] It must be remembered, however, that, according to Aristotle, the copper of the Mossynœci in Northern Asia Minor was brilliant and white, owing to its mixture with a species of earth, the exact nature of which was kept a secret. The Babylonian ideograph for "bronze," therefore, may have been a similar kind of hardened copper, which was transferred to denote "bronze" when the alloy of copper and tin became known.

[2] See Garstang, *El-Arâbah*, p. 10. Dr. Gladstone, however, after giving the results of his analysis of the Sixth-dynasty copper discovered by Professor Petrie at Dendera, suggests that the small amount of tin observable in it (about one per cent.) may have been added to it artificially (*Dendereh*, p. 61). Bronze was "the normal metal" of the Amorite period at Gezer (Macalister, *Quarterly Statement of the Palestine Exploration Fund*, April 1904, p. 119), and the three cities which represent this period go back beyond the age of the Twelfth Egyptian dynasty, to at least B.C. 2900 (see *Quarterly Statement*, January 1905, pp. 28-9). At Troy also Schliemann found numerous bronze weapons in the Second (prehistoric) city (*Ilios*, pp. 475-9). In Krete bronze daggers of the Early Minoan period (coeval with the Middle Empire of Egypt) have been found at Patema and Agia Triada (*Annual of the British School at Athens*, x. p. 198), and the pottery of the Middle Minoan period (B.C. 2000-1500) was associated at Palaikastro with a bronze button, two miniature bronze sickles, and a pair of bronze tweezers (*ibid.* p. 202). As for the Caucasus, bronze was not known there till a late date. Wilke

become common until the Hyksos predecessors of the Eighteenth dynasty had made themselves masters of the valley of the Nile. From about B.C. 1600 onwards, enormous quantities of it were employed in the eastern basin of the Mediterranean and the adjoining lands, necessitating an equally large supply of tin. What the source of this tin may have been it is not my present purpose to inquire. But the persistence of the copper age in Babylonia, as well as in the tumuli of Askabad, east of the Caspian, indicates that the manufacture of bronze must have migrated from the north-west to the Babylonian plain. We find it first in Assyria, not in Babylonia, and it may well be that the Assyrians derived it from Armenia and the population of Cappadocia, where, as I shall show in a subsequent chapter, they had established colonies at an early period. At all events, the earliest examples of bronze yet met with were discovered by Dr. Schliemann in the Second prehistoric city at Troy.

It was to this region that classical tradition referred the origin of working in iron. An analysis of the gold of the first six Egyptian dynasties submitted to Dr. Gladstone by Professor Petrie proved that it was mixed with silver, and hence must have been derived from Asia Minor.[1] Egyptian legend made "the followers of Horus," who founded dynastic Egypt,

---

(*Zeitschrift für Ethnologie*, 1904, pp. 39–104) has shown that the bronze culture of the Caucasus was derived from the valley of the Danube, and made its way eastward along the northern coast of Pontus ; see also Rössler, *Zeitschrift für Ethnologie*, 1905, p. 118.

[1] *Dendereh* (Egypt Exploration Fund), p. 62, for the gold of the Sixth dynasty ; *The Royal Tombs of the Earliest Dynasties*, pp. 39–40, for that of the First dynasty.

metallurgists and smiths whose metal weapons enabled them to subdue the older neolithic population. The story as it has come down to us declares the smiths to have been workers in iron ; iron, however, must be the substitute of the later version of the story for some other metal, since, though Vyse claims to have discovered an iron clamp in the great pyramid of Giza,[1] and Petrie has found a mass of iron in a Sixth-dynasty deposit in the temple of Osiris at Abydos,[2] ironsmiths can hardly have existed in the pre-dynastic age. It is probable, therefore, that copper was the metal which the dynastic Egyptians introduced into their new home, and which was already in use in Babylonia. But the intercourse with Asia Minor, which the gold of the First dynasty indicates must even then have been going on, makes it possible that it was from this quarter of the world that the earliest knowledge of the manufacture of bronze was brought to the valley of the Nile. Even in the time of the Twelfth dynasty, however, the tools found by Professor Petrie in the workmen's huts at Kahûn are of copper rather than of bronze.[3] The colossal statue of King Pepi of the Sixth dynasty, discovered at Hierakonpolis, is of hammered copper,

---

[1] Vyse, *Pyramids of Gizeh*, i. p. 276. The clamp was actually found by his assistant Hill, after blasting away the two outer stones behind which it had been placed.

[2] *Abydos*, part ii. p. 33. An iron pin of the age of the Eighteenth dynasty was found by Garstang at Abydos (*El-Arâbah*, p. 30).

[3] *Illahun, Kahun and Gurob*, p. 12. Dr. Gladstone's analyses give only about 2 parts of tin to 96·35 of copper. The bronze of the Eighteenth dynasty found at Gurob yielded a less proportion of tin (about 7 parts to 90 of copper) than the bronze of the Second Assyrian Empire. A ring of pure tin, however, was also discovered at Gurob.

and we have to wait for the advent of the Eighteenth dynasty before bronze becomes the predominant metal. That such was the case points to the Hyksos period as that in which bronze succeeded in superseding the older copper. It may be that the Hyksos brought the extended use of it with them from Syria. In Southern Palestine, Mr. Macalister's excavations at Gezer have shown that bronze rather than copper was largely employed throughout the so-called Amorite period, which went back to an earlier age than that of the Twelfth dynasty, and it is just here that in the time of the Eighteenth dynasty bronze itself began to make way for iron. Mr. J. L. Myres has recently traced the polychrome pottery of Southern Canaan to the Hittite lands of Cappadocia,[1] where the red ochre was found by which it was characterized, and a knowledge of bronze may have travelled along the same road.

But these are speculations which may or may not be verified by future research. For the present we must be content with the fact that, in spite of the philological evidence to the contrary, copper, and not bronze, was the metal which preceded the use of iron in Babylonia, whereas in the northern kingdom of Assyria bronze was already known at a comparatively early date. So far as the existing evidence can carry us, it seems to indicate that Babylonia was the primitive home of the copper industry, while bronze, on the other hand, made its way eastward from Asia Minor and the north of Syria. Where bronze was first invented is still un-

[1] *Journal of the Anthropological Institute*, xxxiii. pp. 367 *sqq.*

known to us ; all that seems certain is that it must
have been in a land where copper and tin are found
together.

NOTE

According to the mineralogists, in the western part
of the northern hemisphere tin is found only in Britain,
Spain and the neighbourhood of Askabad, the scanty
surface-tin of Saxony, France and Tuscany being too
poor and insignificant to have attracted attention in
antiquity (see de Morgan, *Mission Scientifique au
Caucase*, ii. pp. 16–28). The American excavations at
Askabad under Professor Pumpelly appear to have
made it clear that bronze was not invented in that
part of the world, or indeed used in early days, and
we are thus thrown back on Britain and Spain. It is
quite certain, however, that bronze made its way to
the west of Europe from the east, and the Hon. John
Abercromby has proved (*Journal of the Anthropological
Institute*, xxxii. pp. 375–94, and *Proceedings of Society
of Antiquaries of Scotland*, 1903–4, pp. 323–410) that
the bronze culture came to this country from the
valley of the central Rhine where it cuts the river at
Mayence. On the other hand, the bronze-age civilization of the Danube valley, the Balkan peninsula and
Italy forms a whole with that of the south-eastern
basin of the Mediterranean, which again is closely
connected with the bronze-age culture of the Ægean,
Asia Minor and Egypt, while the civilization of the
Danube valley leads on to that of Central Europe,
and, to a less extent, of Scandinavia and Northern
Germany. Montelius (*Journal of the Anthropological*

Institute, 1900, pp. 89 *sqq.*) has pointed out that the early bronze culture of Northern Italy was carried to Scandinavia along the route of the amber trade as far back as the close of the neolithic age in Sweden, and the numerous objects of Irish gold found in Scandinavia—though, it is true, of somewhat later date—show that commercial relations must have existed between the British Islands and the Scandinavian peninsula. Tin might have followed the gold route until it met the amber route, by which it would have been carried southward to Central Europe and the Adriatic.

In Western Europe the sword, like the socketed celt, is first met with in the third and last period into which the bronze age has been divided. The earliest examples of the sword, in fact, are those discovered at Mykenæ, which belong to the age of the Eighteenth Egyptian dynasty. Schliemann found only the dirk at Troy, and, so far as our present evidence goes, the dirk alone was used by the Hittites and Proto-Armenians down to the seventh century B.C. The scimitar, however, was known in Assyria and at Gezer at least as early as the fourteenth century B.C. (see p. 57 above), and in Cyprus the sword makes its appearance along with the knife and fibula in the later bronze age after the close of the age of copper. Similarly in Krete it was only in tombs of the Late Mykenæan (or Late Minoan) period that the cemetery of Knossos yielded swords of bronze (*Annual of the British School at Athens*, x. p. 4). The dirk of the copper age was stanged as at Troy and in the Danube valley, the Cyprian and Hungarian forms being practically identical. From the Danube valley the stanged

E

spear-head passed to Western Europe during the second period of the bronze age. The fibula is not found at Troy, where the early bronze age will have corresponded with the copper age of Cyprus. All this goes to show (1) that the scimitar—the *harpê* of the Perseus myth—was a Semitic invention, while the long sword was of European origin ; (2) that at Troy, and possibly also in Southern Palestine, to which Hittite polychrome pottery was carried at an early date, bronze was known at a time when only copper was used in Cyprus and Egypt; and (3) that the characteristic weapon of this primitive bronze age was the dirk, which continued to characterize Asia Minor long after the sword and scimitar had been invented elsewhere. Taken in connection with the fact that the pottery and decorative designs of Asia Minor can be linked with those of the Balkan peninsula and the valley of the Danube, we may provisionally conclude that Northern Asia Minor was the home of the invention of bronze. Against this is the fact that no tin has hitherto been found there, and we should accordingly have to explain the origin of bronze by the theory that after the discovery of various processes for hardening copper, further experiments were made with imported tin. Unfortunately, neither the south of Cornwall nor Asia Minor, with the exception of the Troad, has as yet been scientifically explored from an archæological point of view. But it deserves mention that the curious needles with a double head of twisted wire, which are met with among the remains of the bronze age in Britain, are characteristic of the copper age in Cyprus and of the early bronze age at Troy.

CHAPTER III

THE SUMERIANS

AMONG the first results of the decipherment of the Assyrian cuneiform inscriptions was one which was so unexpected and revolutionary, that it was received with incredulity and employed to pour discredit on the fact of the decipherment itself. European scholars had long been nursing the comfortable belief that the white race primarily, and the natives of Europe secondarily, were *ipso facto* superior to the rest of mankind, and that to them belonged of right the origin and development of civilization. The discovery of the common parentage of the Indo-European languages had come to strengthen the belief; the notion grew up that in Sanskrit we had found, if not the primeval language, at all events a language that was very near to it, and idyllic pictures were painted of the primitive Aryan community living in its Asiatic home and already possessed of the elements of its later culture. Outside and beyond it were the barbarians, races yellow and brown and black, with oblique eyes and narrow foreheads, whose intelligence was not much above that of the brute beasts. Such culture as some of them may have had was derived from the white race, and perhaps spoilt in the borrowing. The idea of the rise of a civilization outside the limits of the white race was regarded as a paradox.

It was just this paradox to which the first decipherers of Assyrian cuneiform found themselves forced. And another paradox was added to it. Not only had the civilization of the Euphrates and Tigris originated amongst a race that spoke an agglutinative language, and therefore was neither Aryan nor Semitic, the civilization of the Semitic Babylonians and Assyrians was borrowed from this older civilization along with the cuneiform system of writing. It seemed impossible that so revolutionary a doctrine could be true, and Semitic philologists naturally denounced it. For centuries Hebrew had been supposed to have been the language of Paradise, and the old belief which made the Semitic Adam the first civilized man still unconsciously affected the Semitic scholars of the nineteenth century. It was hard to part with the prejudices of early education, especially when they were called upon to do so by a small group of men whose method of decipherment was an enigma to the ordinary grammarian, and who were introducing new and dangerous principles into the study of the extinct Semitic tongues.

The method of decipherment was nevertheless a sound one, and the result, which seemed so incredible and impossible when first announced, is now one of the assured facts of science. The first civilized occupants of the alluvial plain of Babylonia were neither Semites nor Aryans, but the speakers of an agglutinative language, and to them were due all the elements of the Babylonian culture of later days. It was they who first drained the marshes, and regulated the course of the rivers by canals, thereby transforming what had been a pestiferous swamp into the most fertile of lands ; it was they who founded the great cities of the country, and invented the pictorial characters, the cursive forms of which became what we term cuneiform. The theology and law of later Babylonia went back to them, and long after Semitic Babylonian had become the language of the country, legal judgments were still written in the old language and the theological literature was still studied in it. The Church and the Law were as loth to give up the dead language of Sumer as they were in modern Europe to give up the use of Latin.

This dead agglutinative language has been called sometimes Akkadian, sometimes Sumerian, but Sumerian is the name which has been finally selected. In fact, this was the name applied to it by the Semitic Babylonians themselves, who included in the term the two dialects—or rather the two forms of the language at different periods of its development—which have been preserved to us in the cuneiform tablets. Strictly speaking, the dialect which had been most affected by contact with the Semites, and had in consequence suffered most from phonetic decay, was known as the language of Akkad, but this was because Akkad represented Northern Babylonia, which had become Semitic at an earlier date than the south and had been the seat of the first great Semitic Empire.[1] Both

[1] The two dialects were called *eme*-KU (i.e. *eme-lakhkha*, W.A.I. iii. 4, 31, 32), "the language of the enchanter," and *eme*-SAL "the woman's language," which are rendered in Semitic Babylonian, *lisan Sumeri* and (*lisan*) *Akkadi*, "the language of Sumer" and "the language of Akkad." In a tablet (81, 7–27, 130, 6, 7) they are said to be "like" one another. Other dialects were

names, Akkadian and Sumerian, are correct as applied to the primitive language of Chaldæa, but of the two Sumerian is preferable, not only because it was used by the Babylonian scribes themselves, but also because it denoted the oldest and purest form of the language before it had passed under foreign influence.

This, then, was the great archæological fact which resulted from the decipherment of the Assyro-Babylonian texts. The earliest civilized inhabitants of Babylonia did not speak a Semitic language, and therefore presumably they were not Semites. It is perfectly true that language and race are not synonymous terms, and that we are seldom justified in arguing from the one to the other. But the Sumerian language is one of the exceptions which proves the rule. Those who spoke it were the first civilizers of Western Asia, the inventors and perfecters of a system of writing which was destined to be one of the chief humanizing agents of the ancient world, the authors of the irrigation engineering of the Babylonian plain, and the builders of its many cities. The language they spoke, accordingly, could not have been forced upon them by conquerors who have otherwise left no trace behind them, and they certainly would not have exchanged it of their own accord for their native tongue. The Semitic languages have always been conspicuous for the tenacity with which they

---

termed "the language of the sacrificer" and "the language of the anointer," as being used by these two classes of priests. They differed, perhaps, from the standard dialects in intonation or the use of technical words. We hear also of "a carter's language" in which *anbarri*—which, it is noticeable, is a Sumerian word—meant "yoke and reins," *i.e.* "harness" (*Zeitschrift für Assyriologie*, ix. p. 164).

have held their own, and the conservatism with which they have resisted change. We may still hear in the Egyptian Arabic of to-day the very words which were written by Semitic Babylonian scribes upon their tablets some four or five thousand years ago. A Semitic people would have been the last to borrow the language of its less-civilized neighbours without any assignable reason. The fact, consequently, that the pioneers of Babylonian culture spoke an agglutinative language fully justifies us in concluding that they belonged to a race that was not Semitic.

Sumerian, however, was not the only language in the neighbourhood of the Babylonian plain which was agglutinative. Further to the east, in the highlands of Elam, other agglutinative languages were spoken, monuments of one or more of which have been preserved to us. Whether or not the agglutinative languages of Elam were related to the Sumerian of Babylonia, I cannot tell ; so far as our materials go at present they do not warrant us in saying more than that, like Sumerian, they were of the agglutinative type. It is only rarely that the scientific philologist is able to separate some of the multitudinous languages of the globe into genealogically related groups ; for the most part they stand isolated and apart from one another, and, however much we may wish to group them together, it is seldom that we find such proofs of a common descent as will satisfy the requirements of science. Families of speech—or at all events such as can be scientifically proved to be so—are the exception and not the rule.

Eastward of Sumer the type of language was thus agglutinative, as it was in Sumer itself. And in the days when civilization first grew up there, there is no sign or trace of the languages we call inflectional. The speakers of Aryan dialects, whom we find in classical times in Media or Persia or North-Western India, belong to a later epoch; the old belief in the Asiatic cradle of the Aryan tongues has long since been given up by the anthropologist and comparative philologist,[1] and it is recognized that if we are to look for it anywhere it must be in Eastern Europe. The Semitic languages are equally absent; the tide of Semitic speech which eventually overflowed Babylonia, surged northward and eastward into Assyria and Elam, but never succeeded in passing Susiana, and was finally driven again from the ground it had once gained there. The home of the Semite lay to the west and not to the east of the Babylonian plain. Babylonian culture owed its origin to a race whose type of language was that of the Finn, of the Magyar or the Japanese.

The physical characteristics of this race cannot as yet be fully determined. The oldest sculptures yielded by Babylonian excavation belong to a time when the Semite was already in the land. It might be supposed that the early monuments of Tello, which were erected by Sumerian princes and go back to Sumerian times, would give us the necessary materials ; but not only are they too rude and infantile to be of scientific use, they also indicate the existence of two ethnological types, one heavily bearded, the other beardless, with oblique eyes and negrito-like face. It is not until we come to the age of Semitic domina-

----

[1] Fick, however, is an exception (*Beiträge zur Kunde der indogermanischen Sprachen*, xxix. pp. 229-247.

tion that sculpture is sufficiently realistic for exact anthropological purposes. At the same time, there was to the last a marked contrast of both form and feature in the artistic representation of the Babylonian and his more purely Semitic Assyrian neighbour. The squat, thick figure, the full, well-shaven cheeks, the large, almond-shaped eyes and round head of King Merodach-nadin-akhi in the twelfth century B.C. still reproduce the characteristic form and features of the statues found in the palace of Gudea, the Sumerian high-priest of Lagas, who lived more than a thousand years before. The aquiline or hooked nose, the thick lips and muscular limbs which distinguished the Assyrian are generally wanting in Babylonia. And, on the other hand, there is a likeness between the Babylonian as he is portrayed on the monuments and the Elamite adversaries of Assur-bani-pal, some of whom, it is noticeable, are depicted with beards, though the excavations of Dieulafoy and de Morgan at Susa have shown (according to Quatrefages and Hamy) that a beardless and short-nosed negrito type with round heads was aboriginal in Elam. The same type is reproduced in one of the heads found at Tello, and M. de Morgan has pointed out that similar brachycephalic and beardless negritos are represented on the monuments of Naram-Sin as serving in the army of Akkad.[1] We may conclude, therefore, that they still formed a part of the population of Northern Babylonia even in the age when it had passed com-

---

[1] *Mémoires de la Délégation en Perse*, i. pp. 152-3. Photographs of the two types—Sumerian and Semitic—represented on the early monuments of Babylonia are given by Dr. Pinches in an interesting Paper in the *Journal of the Royal Asiatic Society*, January 1900, pp. 87-93.

pletely under Semitic rule.   Indeed, Dr. Pinches has shown that the pure Semitic type is not depicted in Babylonian art, outside the kingdom of Akkad, "before the time of the First dynasty of Babylon, which began to reign about B.C. 2300."

It has often been maintained that the Sumerians themselves were an immigrant people, who had descended from the mountains of Elam.   There is nothing unreasonable in the supposition; it was always difficult to prevent the mountaineers of Elam from making raids in Babylonia, and one of their tribes succeeded in settling in the country and establishing at Babylon one of the longest-lived of its dynasties.   But the supposition mainly rests upon two facts.   The pictorial hieroglyphs out of which the cuneiform characters have developed had no special sign for "river," while the same character represented both "mountain" and "country."   It would seem, therefore, that the land in which the cuneiform system of writing was first invented was just the converse of the Babylonian plain, being at once mountainous and riverless.   That the same character means both "mountain" and "country" is no doubt a strong argument in favour of the Elamite origin of Babylonian civilization.   That the use of the primitive hieroglyphs should have survived in Elam while it was lost in Babylonia, as M. de Morgan's discoveries have shown to be the case, is also another fact which may perhaps be claimed on the same side; at any rate it indicates that they were known to the Elamites before the cursive cuneiform had developed out of them.   But the want of a special character for "river" is not so decisive as it appears at

first sight to be. The word " river " is represented by
two ideographic signs which literally signify " the
watery deep," and so point to the fact that those who
originally invented them lived not in the highlands
of the East, but on the shores of that Persian Gulf
which the Babylonians of the historic period still
called " the deep." As it was also known as " the
salt river," it is not difficult to understand how, to
those whose experience of navigable water had
been confined to the Persian Gulf, the Tigris and
Euphrates would have seemed but repetitions of the
Gulf on a smaller scale.[1]

The rise of Sumerian culture on the shores of
the Persian Gulf is in accordance with Babylonian
tradition. Babylonian myths told how Oannes or Ea,
the god of culture, had risen each morning out of his
palace in " the deep," bringing with him the elements
of civilization which he communicated to mankind.
Letters, science and art had all been his gifts. He
had instructed the wild tribes of the coast to build
houses and erect temples ; he had compiled for
them the first law-book, and had instructed them in
the mysteries of agriculture. Babylonian civilization
was sea-born. The system of cosmology which
finally won its way to acceptance with the priesthood
and philosophers of Babylonia was one which had
been first conceived at Eridu, the site of which is
now more than a hundred miles distant from the

[1] It is noticeable that the script of the other people whose
civilization grew up on the banks of a river, the Egyptians
namely, contains no special ideograph for " river." The word
is expressed by the phonetically-written *atur*, with the determinative of " water " or " irrigation basin." As in the primitive
hieroglyphs of Babylonia, " the sea " was a " circle."

sea, but in the early days of Babylonian history, before the silting up of the shore, had been its seaport. Here the first man Adam[1] was supposed to have lived, and to have spent his time fishing in the waters of the Gulf. The whole earth was believed to have grown out of a primeval deep like the mudflats which the inhabitants of Eridu saw slowly emerging from the retreating sea. Philosophy and cosmology, with the theology with which they were associated, looked back upon Eridu and the Babylonian coast as their primeval home.[2]

In fact the physical conditions of the Babylonian plain rendered it impossible for the first culture of the country to have sprung up in it. Before it was reclaimed by engineering skill and labour the larger part of it had been a pestiferous marsh. The science needed for making it habitable, at least by civilized man, must have arisen outside its boundaries. Only when he was already armed with a civilization which enabled him to dig canals, to mould bricks, and pile his houses and temples on artificial foundations could the Sumerian have settled in the Babylonian plain and there developed it still further. The cities of the plain grew up each round its sanctuary, which became a centre of civilization and progress, of agriculture and trade. But the builders of the sanctuaries must have brought their culture with them from elsewhere.

Of these sanctuaries the most venerable was that of Bel the Elder at Nippur. It has been systematically excavated by the Americans down to its founda-

---

[1] For proof of this reading see *Expository Times*, xvii. p. 416 and note *infra*, p. 91.
[2] See my *Religions of Ancient Egypt and Babylonia*, pp. 373-84.

tions, and the successive strata of its history laid bare. Inscribed objects have been found in all the strata, carrying the history of the cuneiform system of writing back to the days when the temple was originally built. But it is still the cuneiform system of writing as far back as we can go, that is to say the characters are the cursive forms of earlier hieroglyphic pictures, the features of which are in most cases scarcely traceable. Here and there, it is true, the primitive pictorial form has been preserved, but this is the exception and not the rule. As a rule the earliest writing found at Nippur, and coeval with the foundation of its temple, is already the degenerated and cursive hand which we call cuneiform.

The fact is very noteworthy. The cuneiform characters have assumed the shapes which give them their name owing to their having been inscribed on clay by a stylus of wood or metal, which obliged the writer to substitute a series of wedge-like indentations for curves and straight lines. As time went on, the number of the wedges was reduced, the forms of the characters were simplified, and the resemblance to the pictures they were once intended to represent became more and more indistinct. The cuneiform script is, in short, a running hand, like the hieratic of Egypt. But whereas in Egypt the hieratic running hand does not come into common use until long after the beginning of the monumental period, while the pictorial hieroglyphs continued to be employed to the last, in Babylonia the cuneiform running hand has superseded the primeval pictures as far back as our records carry us. When the temple of Nippur was built—and it was probably one of the first, if not the first, to be built in the Babylonian plain—the clay tablet was already in use for writing purposes, and the cursive cuneiform had taken the place of the older hieroglyphs.

The Babylonian plain was called by its Sumerian inhabitants the Edin, or "Plain," a name which was borrowed by the Semites and has been made familiar to us by the book of Genesis. Originally it had meant all the uncultivated flats on either side of the Euphrates, but it soon acquired the sense of the country as opposed to the city, and so of the cultivated plain itself. Most of the important Babylonian cities were built in it between the Euphrates on the west and the Tigris on the east. A few only lay beyond it on the western bank of the Euphrates. One of these was Eridu, another was Ur, a third was Borsippa.

Of Eridu I have already spoken. Some six or eight thousand years ago it was the sea-port of primitive Babylonia.[1] Ur, which stood close to it, seems to have been a colony of Nippur, and therefore of comparatively late origin.[2] Borsippa was a small and unimportant town, which eventually became a suburb of Babylon, and Babylon, on the eastern bank of the Euphrates, was itself a colony of Eridu.[3] Hence of the cities which stood outside the Edin of Babylonia, and may therefore belong to an age when

[1] Taylor found quantities of sea-shells in its ruins (*Journal of the Royal Asiatic Society*, xv. p. 412). At the time of its foundation an arm of the sea probably ran up to it from the south-east, though the myth of Adamu describes him as fishing each day in the waters of the actual Gulf, rather than in an arm of it.

[2] The Moon-god of Ur was a "son" of El-lil, the god of Nippur.

[3] For proof of this see my *Religion of the Ancient Babylonians* p. 105.

Babylonian civilization was still in its infancy, Eridu alone is of account. And the priority even of Eridu was contested. Traditionally Sippara, which is expressly stated to have been in "the Edin," claimed to be the oldest of Babylonian cities ; one quarter of it bore the name of " Sippara that is from everlasting," and like Eridu, it believed itself to have been the abode of the first man.[1] Thus far, however, the monuments have given us nothing to substantiate the claim; the culture-god of Babylonia was Ea of Eridu, not the Sun-god of Sippara, and for the present, therefore, we must look to the shore of the Persian Gulf, rather than to the "land of Eden" for the cradle of Babylonian civilization.

At any rate, both Sippara and Eridu were of Sumerian foundation, as indeed were nearly all the great cities of Babylonia. Eridu was a later form of the older Eri-dugga, "the good city," a name which seems to have been the starting-point of more than one legend. The growth of the coast to the south of it gives us some idea as to the age to which its foundation must reach back.

[1] A tablet obtained by Dr. Hayes Ward divides Sippara into four quarters, "Sippara of Eden," " Sippara that is from everlasting," " Sippara of the Sun-god," and " Sippara," which may be the "Sippara of Anunit " or " Sippara of Aruru," the creatress of man, of other inscriptions. Amelon or Amelu, "man," who corresponds with the Enos of Scripture, is said in the fragments of Berossus to have belonged to Pantibibla, or " Book-town," and since Euedoranchus of Pantibibla, the counterpart of the Biblical Enoch, is the monumental Enme-dhur-anki of Sippara, it is clear that Pantibibla is a play on the supposed signification of Sippara (from *sipru*, "a writing" or "book"). The claim to immemorial antiquity made on behalf of Sippara may be due to the fact that Akkad, the seat of the first Semitic empire, was either in the immediate neighbourhood of Sippara or another name of one of the four quarters of Sippara itself.

It was, as I have said, the primitive sea-port of Babylonia, and its legend of the first man Adamu made him a fisherman in the Persian Gulf. Its site is now rather more than a hundred miles distant from the present line of coast. The progress of alluvial deposit brought down by the Euphrates and Tigris can be estimated by the fact that forty-seven miles of it have been formed since Spasinus Charax, the modern Mohammerah, was built in the age of Alexander the Great, and was for a time the port of Chaldæa. During the last 2000 years, accordingly, the rate of deposit would seem to have been about 115 feet a year. This, however, does not agree with the observations of Loftus, who made the rate not more than a mile in every seventy years,[1] while on the other hand Sir Henry Rawlinson adduced reasons for believing it to have been more rapid in the past than it is to-day, and that consequently the rate must once have been as much as a mile in thirty years.[2] It is desirable

---

[1] *Chaldæa and Susiana,* p. 282.

[2] *Journal of the Royal Geographical Society,* xxvii. p. 186. Rawlinson calculated the rate of advance from that made by the Babylonian Delta between 1793 and 1833. In the age of Strabo and Arrian the Tigris and Euphrates were not yet united, while in the time of Nearchus (B.C. 335) the mouth of the Euphrates was 345 miles from Babylon. De Morgan calculates that between the age of Nearchus and that of Sennacherib, when the Euphrates had not yet joined the more rapid Tigris, the rate of increase must have been much slower than it is to-day and have not exceeded eighty metres a year. In the age of Sennacherib Eridu was already seventy miles distant from the coast (de Morgan, *Mémoires de la Délégation en Perse,* i. pp. 5–23). The distance from the Shatt el-Arab (the united stream of the Tigris and Euphrates) to the end of the alluvium in the Persian Gulf is 277 kilometres, or 172 miles. Some idea of the appearance of the coast in the Abrahamic age may be gained from the map of the world drawn by a Babylonian tourist in the time of

that some competent geologist should study the question on the spot. Taking, however, as a basis of calculation, the one known fact of the rate of growth since the foundation of Spasinus Charax, and bearing in mind that before the junction of the Tigris and Euphrates the rate of advance must have been comparatively slow, we should have to go back to about B.C. 5000 as the latest date at which Eridu could still have been the sea-port of the country.

Was it here that the system of writing which was so closely entwined with the origin of Babylonian civilization was first invented? Babylonian tradition in later days certainly believed that such was the case, and the fact that Ea of Eridu was the culture-god of Babylonia is strongly in its favour. But there are difficulties in the way. Eridu was the home of the "white witchcraft" of early Chaldæa; it was here that the charms and incantations were composed which gave the priesthood of Eridu its influence, and made the god they worshipped the impersonation of wisdom. The belief that he was the originator of Babylonian culture may have had its source in the system of magic which was associated with his name. Eridu was built on the Semitic side of the Euphrates, and the Semitic tribes who received their letters and their civilization from the Sumerians of Eridu would naturally have looked upon the city of their teachers as the primeval home of Sumerian culture. The traditions that made Eridu the starting-point of Sumerian civilization could thus be explained away,

---

Khammu-rabi which I have published in the *Expository Times*, November 1906.

and we should be left free to settle the question of its origin upon purely archæological evidence.

Unfortunately the site of Eridu has not yet been systematically excavated. Once again the archæological materials for settling an archæological question are not at hand, and we are thrown back upon an examination of the picture-writing from which the cuneiform characters are derived. Here the evidence on the whole may be said to be in favour of tradition. It is true that there is no special ideograph for " river," but there is one for " the deep," and " the spirit of the deep " must have been a chief object of worship at the time when the primitive hieroglyphs were first formed. The " ship," too, played a prominent part in the life of their inventors, and the picture of it represented it as moved not by oars but by a sail.[1]   The flowering reed was equally prominent, and was even used to symbolize what stood firm and established.[2]   Houses, fortresses, temples, and cities were built of brick, and vases were moulded out of clay.[3]   The tablet, rectangular or square, was already employed for the purpose of writing, but as it was provided with a

[1] There is a striking resemblance between the primitive Babylonian picture of a boat and the sailing boat depicted on the prehistoric pottery of Egypt, for which last see Capart, *Les Débuts de l'Art en Egypte*, p. 116.

[2] Perhaps, however, this was really due to the accidental similarity of sound between *gi*, "a reed," and *gin*, "to be firm."

[3] The various forms of vases represented in the early pictography are given by de Morgan in a very instructive article, " Sur les procédès techniques en usage chez les scribes babyloniens," in the *Recueil des Travaux relatifs à la Philologie et à l'Archéologie égyptiennes*, xxvii. 3, 4 (1905). Among special vases were those for oil, wine and honey. The butter or oil jar was closed with a clay sealing exactly like those of early Egypt. Vases with spouts were also used.

handle or a couple of rings at the top, I think it was more probably of wood than of clay. The sheep, goat and ox were domesticated,[1] and so also probably was the ass,[2] and corn was cultivated in the fields. The symbol of the "earth" appears to have been the picture of an island of circular or elliptical form. Among trees the cedar was well known.

All this points to the sea-coast of Babylonia as the district in which its civilization first arose. But on the other hand, there is the fact that "country" and "mountain" are alike represented by the picture of a mountainous land. There is also the fact that the land in which the inventors of the hieroglyphs lived was one in which copper, gold and silver were procurable—perhaps also meteoric iron ; and the further fact that hard wood was sufficiently plentiful for tools or weapons to have been made of it before the employment of metal. That they should have been made of wood, however, and not of stone, is a strong argument in favour of the Babylonian coast.

It is on wood, moreover, that the first hieroglyphs must have been painted or cut. Many of them represented round objects or were formed of curved lines, which were transformed into a series of wedge-like indentations when imprinted by a stylus upon clay. We know, therefore, that clay was not the original writing material ; its use as such, in fact, is coeval with the rise of that cursive script which, in the case

---

[1] The American excavations at Askabad have shown that the domestication of animals, including the camel, took place during the neolithic age, the goat being one of the last to be tamed.

[2] This, however, is not absolutely certain, since the ideograph which denotes an "ass" originally signified merely "a yoked beast."

of the Egyptian hieroglyphics, is called hieratic, but in Assyro-Babylonian is known as cuneiform. It was the attempt to reproduce the old pictures upon clay that created the cuneiform characters. As metal is not likely to have been employed by the primitive scribes of Chaldæa, and there is no trace of stone having been used—even the stone cylinder of later days being called a *dup-sar* or " written tablet "—we are left to choose between wood and papyrus. In favour of papyrus is the fact that the circular forms of so many of the pictures suggest that they were originally painted rather than engraved ; on the other hand, it is doubtful whether the papyrus grows in the Babylonian rivers, or at any rate did so in the prehistoric age. And the pictograph of a " written document " is not a strip or roll of papyrus, as in Egypt, but a tablet with a handle or loop. It is true that the primeval picture which denoted " copper " has much the same form, but as even cutting instruments had the determinative of " wood " attached to them in the early picture writing, it is clear that the original tablet could not have been of metal, whatever might have been the case with its later successors. The picture, moreover, of the " tablet " is distinguished from that of a " plate of bronze " by the addition of a string which is tied to the handle.

On the whole, therefore, the only archæological evidence available at present is on the side of the tradition which made Babylonian culture move northward from the coast. The only fact against it of which I know is that, as I have already stated, the word for land was symbolized by the picture of a triple mountain. But this fact is not insuperable.

Before the silting up of the shore, the old coast-line of Babylonia would have stretched away north-eastward of Eridu towards the mountains of Elam. Whether the mountains that fringed what would then have been the eastern coast of the Persian Gulf are visible from the site of Eridu, I do not know; if the clear light of Upper Egypt exists there they would be so. Nor do I know whether on the western side there are mountain ranges visible in Arabia; these are points which can be cleared up only when the country has been thoroughly explored.

Eridu lay five miles southward of Ur,[1] that "Ur of the Chaldees" from which Hebrew history affirmed the ancestor of the nation had come. Ur was never a maritime port like Eridu; it stood on the Arabian plateau and looked towards the west. Its face was turned to the Semitic rather than to the Sumerian world. From the first, therefore, it must have been in touch with Semitic tribes. And a curious reminiscence of the fact survived in the western Semitic languages. Ur or Uru signifies "the city"; it was a Sumerian word, another form of which was *eri*. The word was borrowed by the Semites, and in the Hebrew of the Old Testament, accordingly, the idea of "city" is expressed by *'ir*. The Assyrians of the north, whose vocabulary was otherwise so full of Sumerian loan-words, preferred the native *âlu*, "a tent," to which the meaning of "city" was assigned when Sumerian culture had been passed on to the Semitic race and the tent had been exchanged for the city. The history of the word is a history of early culture as well.

But I am far from saying that it was through Ur that

[1] Peters, *Nibpur*, ii. p. 299.

the civilization of Sumer came to be handed on to its Semitic neighbours. On the contrary, such facts as there are point in a different direction. Western Semites, whom linguistically we may call Arabs or Aramæans, or Canaanites or Hebrews, doubtless mingled with the Sumerian population of Ur, and adopted more or less of its manners and civilization, but it was further north, in the Babylonian Eden itself, that the Semite first came under the influence of the higher culture, and soon outstripped his masters in the arts of life.

The entrance of the Semitic element into Babylonia is at present one of the most obscure of problems. All we can be sure of are certain main facts. First of all, as we have seen, the early culture of Babylonia, including so integral a part of it as the script, was of Sumerian origin. So, too, were the great cities and sanctuaries of the country, as well as the system of irrigation engineering which first made it habitable. Sumerian long continued to be the language of theology and law ; indeed a large part of the Babylonian pantheon of later days was frankly non-Semitic. As was inevitable under such conditions, the Assyrian language contained an immense number of words— many of them compound—which were borrowed from the older language, and its idioms and grammar equally showed signs of Sumerian influence. I have sometimes been tempted, from a scientific point of view, to speak of Semitic Babylonian as a mixed language.

On the other hand, if the elements of Babylonian civilization were Sumerian, the superstructure was Semitic. When the Semites entered into the heritage of Sumerian culture, the cuneiform script must have still been in a very inchoate and immature state. Its pictorial ancestry must still have been clear, and no scruples were felt about altering or adding to the characters. The phonetic application of the characters, which was still in its initial stage in the Sumerian period, was developed and carried to perfection by the Semitic scribes, and a very considerable proportion of their values and ideographic meanings is of Semitic derivation. The theological system was transformed, and a new literature and a new art came into existence. As Sumerian words had been borrowed by the Semites, so, too, Semitic words were borrowed by the Sumerians, and it is possible that examples of them may occur in some of the oldest Sumerian texts known to us.[1] The Babylonians of history, in short, were a mixed people; and their culture and language were mixed like our own.

This, then, is one main fact. A second is that the Semitic element first comes to the front in the northern part of Babylonia. It is in Akkad, and not in Sumer, that the first Semitic Empire—that of Sargon the Elder, B.C. 3800—had its seat, and old as that empire is, it presupposes a long preceding period of Semitic settlement and advance in power and civilization. The cuneiform system of writing is already complete and has ceased to be Sumerian,

[1] Thus in the great historical inscription of Entemena, King of Lagas (B.C. 4000), M. Thureau Dangin is probably right in seeing in *dam-kha-ra* (col. i. 26) a Semitic word. In fact where a word is written syllabically, that is to say phonetically, in a Sumerian text there is an *a priori* probability that it is a loan-word.

archive-chambers of Semitic literature are founded, and Semitic authority is firmly established from Susa in the east to the Mediterranean in the west. Art is no longer Sumerian, and in the hands of the Semitic subjects of Sargon and his son Naram-Sin has reached a perfection which in certain directions was never afterwards surpassed. The engraved seal-cylinders of the period are the finest that we possess. Naturally the Semitic language has superseded the Sumerian in official documents, and the physical type as represented on the monuments is also distinctly Semitic. At the beginning of the fourth millennium before our era, the civilization and culture of Northern Babylonia have thus ceased to be Sumerian, and the sceptre has fallen into the hands of a Semitic race.

But there is a third fact. The displacement of the Sumerian by the Semite was the case only in Northern Babylonia. In the south, in the land of Sumer, the older population continued to be dominant. Sumerian dynasties continued to rule there from time to time, and the old agglutinative language continued to be spoken. When a West-Semitic dynasty governed the country about B.C. 2200, state proclamations and similar official documents had still to be drawn up in the two languages, Semitic Babylonian and Sumerian. Sumerian did not become extinct till a later day. Indeed, after the fall of the empire of Sargon of Akkad there seems to have been a Sumerian reaction. While Susa was lost to the Semites and became the capital of a non-Semitic people who spoke an agglutinative language, the power of the Sumerian princes in Southern Babylonia appears to have revived. At all events even the dynasty which followed that of the

West-Semites bore Sumerian names.[1] It was only under the foreign domination of the Kassites, apparently, who governed Babylonia for nearly 600 years, that the Sumerian element finally became merged in the Semitic and the Babylonian of later history was born.

The last fact is that while what we call Assyrian is Semitic Babylonian with a few dialectal variations, it stands apart from the other Semitic languages. A scientific comparison of its grammar with those of the sister-tongues leads us to believe that it represents one of the two primeval dialects of the Semitic family of speech, the other dialect being that which subsequently split up into the varying dialects of Canaanite or Hebrew, Arabic, South-Arabic and Aramæan—or, adopting the genealogical form of linguistic relationship, Assyro-Babylonian would have been one daughter of the primitive parent-speech, while the other daughter comprised the remaining Semitic languages.[2] There are two conclusions to be drawn from this; one is that the Babylonian Semites must have separated from their kinsfolk and come under Sumerian influence at a very early period, the other that they moved northward, along the banks of the Tigris into Assyria.

With these two inferences we have to be content. Upon the first home of the Semitic race or its affinities with other branches of the white race,

---

[1] This may of course have been only a literary archaism. But if the kings were really of Semitic origin, it is difficult to understand why they should have been ashamed of being called by their native Semitic names.

[2] See Hommel, *Grundriss der Geographie und Geschichte des Alten Orients,* i. pp. 79–82.

Babylonia can naturally throw no light. The earliest glimpses we catch of the Semites of Babylonia are those of a people who have already come under the influences of Sumerian civilization, who are mingling with their teachers and helping with them to build up the stately edifice of historical Babylonia. There were ruder Semitic tribes, it is true, who continued to live their own nomad life on the western bank of the Euphrates or in the marshes that bordered the Persian Gulf. But like the Bedâwîn of to-day on the outskirts of Egypt they were little, if at all, affected by the civilization at their sides. They remained the same wild savages of the desert as their descendants who encamp in the swamps of modern Babylonia; they neither traded nor tilled the ground, and the language they spoke was not the same as that of their Babylonian kindred. They served, however, as the herdsmen and shepherds of their Babylonian neighbours, and the vast flocks whose wool was so important an article of Babylonian trade, were entrusted to their care. But Bedâwîn they were born, and Bedâwîn they continued to be.

Even the Aramæan tribes of the coast-land kept apart from the Babylonians, whether Sumerian or Semitic, until the day when one of their tribes, the Kaldâ or Chaldæans, made themselves masters of Babylon under their prince Merodach-baladan, and from henceforward became an integral factor in the Babylonian population. They must have settled on the borders of Babylonia at a comparatively late date, when Semitic Babylonian had definitely marked itself off from its sister-tongues and the Babylonian Semite had acquired distinctive characteristics of his own. The West-Semitic elements in the population of Babylonia could have entered the country only long after the mixture of Sumerian and Semite had produced the Babylonian of history.

The Babylonian of history came to forget that he had ever had another fatherland than the Babylonian plain, the Eden of the Old Testament, the land whose southern border was formed by "the salt river" or Persian Gulf of early Sumerian geography, with its four branches which were themselves "heads." Here the first man Adamu [1] had been created in Eridu, "the good city," and here therefore the Babylonian Semite placed the home of the first ancestor of his race. But it was a borrowed belief, borrowed along with the other elements of Babylonian culture, and no argument can be drawn from it as to the actual cradle of the Semitic race. Like the story of the deluge, it was part of the Sumerian heritage into which the Semite had entered.

[1] Hitherto read A-da-pa. But the character PA had the value of *mu* when it signified "man," according to a tablet quoted by Fossey, *Contribution au Dictionnaire Sumérien-assyrienne*, No. 2666, and in writing early Babylonian names or words the characters with the requisite phonetic values were selected which harmonized ideographically with the sense of the words. Thus out of the various characters which had the phonetic value of *mu* that was chosen which denoted "man" when the name of the first man was needed to be written. The Semitic Adamu, which M. Thureau Dangin has found used as a proper name in tablets from Tello of the age of Sargon of Akkad, was borrowed from the Sumerian *adam*, which signified "animal," and then, more specifically "man." Thus in the bilingual story of the creation we have (l. 9) *uru nu-dim adam nu-mun-ya*, "a city was not built, a man was not made to stand upright," and a list of slaves published by Dr. Scheil (*Recueil de Travaux*, etc., xx. p. 65) is dated in "the year when Rim-Anum the king (conquered) the land of . . . bi and its inhabitants" (*adam-bi*). See above, p. 76.

The Semitic tradition which made the first man a tiller of the ground may also have been borrowed from the earlier inhabitants of Babylonia. At all events it is significant that the garden in which he was placed was in the land of Eden, and that the picture of a garden or plantation is one of the primitive hieroglyphs of Sumer. The beginnings of Babylonian civilization were bound up with the cultivation of the Babylonian soil; the reclamation of the great alluvial plain was at once the effect and the cause of Sumerian culture. Sumerian culture, in fact, was at the outset essentially that of an agricultural people.

Trade would have come later, when Eridu had become a seaport, and ships ventured on the waters of the Persian Gulf. It grew up under the shelter of the great sanctuaries. Supported at first by the labour of their serfs, the priests in time came to exchange their surplus revenues—the wool of their sheep, the wheat and sesame of their fields, or the wine yielded by their palms—for other commodities, and the temples themselves formed safe and capacious store-houses in which such goods could be kept. In the historical period Babylonia is already a great trading community, and as the centuries passed trade absorbed more and more the energies of its population, agriculture fell into the background, and the Babylonia conquered by Cyrus could be described with truth as "a nation of shopkeepers." Even the crown prince was a merchant who dealt in wool.[1]

The increasing preponderance of trade goes along with the increasing preponderance of the Semitic

[1] *Records of the Past*, New Series, iii. pp. 124-7.

element in the country, and it is tempting to suppose that there was a connection between the two. At present, however, there is no positive evidence that such was the case. Nor is there any positive evidence that the Semites who settled in Babylonia were not already agriculturists. The circumstances in which a people lives are mainly responsible for its being agricultural or pastoral, and the fact that the Bedâwîn neighbours of the Babylonians on the western side of the Euphrates remained a pastoral race does not exclude the possibility that there were other branches of the Semitic family who had already passed out of the pastoral into the agricultural stage before coming into contact with the Sumerians. On the other hand, it is at least noticeable that in Semitic Babylonian the usual word for " city " continued to be one which properly meant a " tent "—the home of the pastoral nomad—and that no Semitic traditions have come down to us of the beginnings of agricultural life outside the limits of the Babylonian " Plain." The title of " Shepherd," moreover, was at times given to the Babylonian kings in days subsequent to the Semitic Empire of Sargon of Akkad. So far as our materials allow us to judge, city-life was the gift of the Sumerian to the primitive Semitic nomad.[1]

To the Semite, however, I believe I have shown in my Lectures on Babylonian religion,[2] we must ascribe an important theological conception. In

---

[1] Erech was one of the earliest of the Semitic settlements in the Babylonian plain, and Erech was known later as 'supuru, " the sheepfold," as is shown by its ideographic equivalent.

[2] *The Religions of Ancient Egypt and Babylonia*, pp. 276-80.

historical Babylonia the gods were conceived of in the form of man. Man was created in the image of God because the gods themselves were men. But the conception cannot be traced back further than the age when the Sumerians and Semites came into contact with one another. In pre-Semitic Sumer there are no anthropomorphic gods. We hear, instead, of the zi or "spirit," a word properly signifying "life" which manifested itself in the power of motion. All things that moved were possessed of life, and there was accordingly a "life" or "spirit" of the water as well as of man or beast. In place of the divine "lord of heaven" whom the Semites adored there was "a spirit of heaven"; in place of Ea, the later Babylonian god of the deep, there was "a spirit of the abyss." Sumerian theology, in fact, was still on the level of animism, and the inventors of the script represented the idea of "god" by the picture of a star. Vestiges of the old animism can still be detected even in the later cult : by the side of the human gods an Assyrian prayer invokes the mountains, the rivers and the winds, and from time to time we come across a worship of deified towns. It was the town itself that was divine, not the deity to whom its chief temple was dedicated. So, again, the god or goddess continued to be symbolized by some sacred animal or object whose figure appears upon seals and boundary-stones, and in some cases we learn that the Sumerian prototypes of the later Babylonian divinities bore such names as "the gazelle," "the antelope" or "the bull."

With the advent of the Semite all is changed. The gods have become men and women with intensified powers and the gift of immortality, but in all other respects they live and act like the men and women of this nether world. Like them, too, they are born and married, and the court of the early prince finds its counterpart in the divine court of the supreme Bel, or " Lord." The Semitic god of Babylon was " lord of gods " and men, of heaven and earth ; Assur of Assyria was " king of the gods " and lord of " the heavenly hosts."

It was natural that, corresponding with this lord of the heavenly hosts, there should be a lord of the hosts of earth, and that as the divine king was clothed in the attributes of man, the human king should take upon him the divine nature. Like the Pharaohs of Egypt or the emperors of Rome, the early kings of Semitic Babylonia were deified. And the deification took place during their life-time,—in fact, so far as we can judge, upon their accession to the throne. In the eyes of their subjects they were incarnate deities, and in their inscriptions they give themselves the title of god. One of them is even called " the god " of Akkad, his capital.[1]

Here, then, in the conception of the divine, we have a clear dividing line between the Semite and his non-Semitic predecessor. So far back as the cuneiform monuments allow us to carry his history, the Semite is anthropomorphic. As a consequence, the gods he worships conform to the social conditions under which he lives. In the desert the sacred stone becomes " the temple of the god " ; in the organized monarchy of Babylonia each deity takes his appointed

[1] See my *Religions of Ancient Egypt and Babylonia*, pp 276–89, 348–61.

place in an imperial court. Under the one supreme ruler there are princes and sub-princes, vice-regents and generals, while angel-messengers carry the commands of Bel to his subjects on earth, like the messengers who carried the letters of the Babylonian king along the high-roads of the empire. On the other hand, the earthly king receives his power and attributes from the god whose adopted son and representative he claims to be. Nowhere has "the divine right of kings" been more fully insisted on than in ancient Babylonia. The laws of the monarch had to be obeyed, foreign nations had to become his vassals, because he was a god on earth as the supreme Bel was god in heaven.

But the reflection of the divine upon the human brought with it not only the exaltation of sovereignty, but also the rise of a priesthood. There were priests of a sort in Sumer of whom many different classes are enumerated. But when we examine the signification of the names attached to them we find that they were not priests in the true sense of the word. They were rather magicians, sorcerers, wizards, masters of charms. They do not develop into priests until after the Semite has entered upon the scene. The god and the priest make their appearance together.

I do not think, however, that we are justified in concluding that the elaborate hierarchy of Babylonia was of purely Semitic origin. On the contrary, like the theological system with which it was associated, it was a composite product. Behind the gods and goddesses of Semitic Babylonia lay the primitive "spirits" and fetishes of Sumer; its mythology and cosmological theories rested on Sumerian foundations; and in the same way the priestly hierarchy was the result of a racial amalgamation in which the Semitic element had adopted and adapted the ideas and institutions of the older people. We do not find the theology and priesthood of Babylonia among other Semitic populations, except where they had been borrowed from the Babylonians (as in Assyria); in the form in which we know them they were peculiarly and distinctively Babylonian. Like the language of Semitic Babylonia, which is permeated with Sumerian elements, or the script, which is a Semitic adaptation of the Sumerian system of writing, they presuppose a mixture of race.

The priesthood eventually proved irreconcilable with "the divine right" of the monarch, though both alike had the same origin. The priests prevailed over the king, and as in England the doctrine of divine right was unable to survive the accession of a German line of princes, so in Babylonia the accession of a foreign, non-Semitic dynasty (that of the Kassites) dealt a death-blow to the belief in a deified king. The king became merely the representative and deputy of the divine "Lord" of heaven, deriving his right to rule from his adoption by the god as a son ; Bel-Merodach came to be regarded as the true ruler of Babylonia, lord of the earth as well as of the heavens, and a theocratic state affords but little room for a secular king. The priests of Bel decided whom their god should recognize or not, and little by little the controlling power of the state passed into their hands It was in a sense a triumph for the non-Semitic element in the population. While the deification of the sovereign may be said to have been purely Semitic in its origin, the necessary corollary of an anthro-

G

pomorphic conception of the deity, the supernatural powers supposed to be inherent in the priesthood went back to Sumerian times. It was because he had once been a master of spells that the priest of the anthropomorphic god could influence the spiritual world. The final triumph of the theocratic principle in Babylonia, where the Semite had been so long dominant, showed that the old racial element was still strong, and ready to reassert itself when the favourable moment arrived. Such, indeed, is generally the history of a mixed people: the conquering or immigrant race may seem to have suppressed or absorbed the earlier population of the country, but as generations pass the foreign element becomes weaker, and the nation in greater or less degree reverts to the older type.

NOTE

So far as the primitive culture of Sumer may be recovered from such of the primitive pictographs as can be at present identified, it may be described as follows. The inventors of them lived on the sea-coast within sight of mountains, but in a marshy district where reeds abounded. Trees also grew there, and the cedar was known. Stone was scarce, but was already cut into blocks and seals. Tablets were used for writing purposes, and copper, gold and silver were worked by the smith. Daggers with metal blades and wooden handles were worn, and copper was hammered into plates, while necklaces or collars were made of gold. Brick was the ordinary building material, and with it cities, forts, temples and houses were constructed. The city was provided with towers and stood on an artificial platform ; the house also had a tower-like appearance. It was provided with a door which turned on a hinge, and could be opened with a sort of key ; the city gate was on a larger scale, and seems to have been double. By the side of the house was an enclosed garden planted with trees and other plants ; wheat and probably other cereals were sown in the fields, and the shadûf was already employed for the purpose of irrigation. Plants were also grown in pots or vases. That floods took place is evident from the existence of a pictograph denoting " inundation," and representing a fish left stranded above the foliage of a tree. Canals or aqueducts had already been dug. The sheep, goat, ox and probably ass had been domesticated, the ox being used for draught, and woollen clothing as well as rugs were made from the wool or hair of the two first. A feathered head-dress was worn on the head. Beds, stools and chairs were used, with carved legs resembling those of an ox. There were fire-places and fire-altars, and apparently chimneys also. Pottery was very plentiful, and the forms of the vases, bowls and dishes were manifold ; there were special jars for honey, butter, oil and wine, which was probably made from dates, and one form of vase had a spout protruding from its side. Some of the vases had pointed feet, and stood on stands with crossed legs ; others were flat-bottomed, and were set on square or rectangular frames of wood. The oil-jars—and probably others also—were sealed with clay, precisely as in early Egypt. Vases and dishes of stone were made in imitation of those of clay, and baskets were woven of reeds or formed of leather. Knives, drills, wedges and an instrument which looks like a saw were all known while bows, arrows and daggers (but not swords nor, probably, spears) were employed in war. Time was reckoned in lunar months. Sacred cakes were offered to the gods, whose images were symbolized sometimes by a bearded human head with a feather crown, sometimes by a two-legged table of offerings on which stand two vases (of incense?). Demons were feared who had wings like a bird, and the foundation stones —or rather bricks—of a house were consecrated by certain objects that were deposited under them. A "year" was denoted by the branch of a tree, as in Egypt, and a "name" by a bird placed over the sacred table of offerings. The country was full of snakes and other creeping things, and wild beasts lurked in the jungle. The pictographs were read from left to right, and various expedients were devised for making them express ideas. Thus *mud*, "to beget," was denoted by the picture of a bird dropping an egg. At other times the pictograph was used to express an idea, the pronunciation of which was the same as that of the object which it represented. The bent knee, for example, was used to express *dug* or *tuk*, "to have," since it represented a "knee," which was called *dug* in Sumerian.

CHAPTER IV

THE RELATION OF BABYLONIAN TO EGYPTIAN CIVILIZATION

In dealing with the question of origins, science is constantly confronted with the problem of unity or polygeneity. Has language one origin or many ; are the various races of mankind traceable to one ancestor or to several ? Do the older civilizations presuppose the same primeval starting-point, or were there independent centres of culture which grew up unknown to one another in different parts of the world ? Under the influences of theology the belief long prevailed that they were all sprung from the same source ; of late the tendency has been in an opposite direction. While the biologist has inclined to a belief in the unity of species, the anthropologist has seen reason to maintain the diversity of origin in culture.

The two earliest civilizations with which we are acquainted were those of Babylonia and Egypt. To a certain extent the conditions under which they both arose were similar. They grew up alike on the banks of great rivers and in a warm, though not tropical, climate. They rested, moreover, on organized systems of agriculture, which again had been made possible by irrigation engineering. In Babylonia the first settlers had found a plain which was little more than a swamp over which the swollen streams of the Euphrates and Tigris wandered at will during the annual period of inundation, and which needed engineering works on a large scale before it could be made habitable. The rivers had to be confined within their channels by means of embankments, and canals had to be cut in order to draw off the surplus supply of water and regulate its distribution to the land. While the swamp was thus being made possible for habitation, the population must have lived on the edge of the desert plateau which bordered it, and have there developed a civilization which not only produced the engineers and their science, but also the concentrated authority which enabled the science to be utilized.

In Egypt it was the banks and delta of the Nile which took the place of the Babylonian plain. Recent discoveries have shown that in the prehistoric age, when the natives still lived in the desert and led a pastoral life, all this was a morass, the haunt of beasts of prey and venomous reptiles. But here again the swamp was rendered habitable by engineering works similar to those of primeval Babylonia. The swamp was transformed into fertile fields, the annual flood of the river was regulated, and an elaborate network of canals and embankments spread over the country. The pastoral nomads of the neolithic age became agriculturists, or were employed in constructing and repairing the works of irrigation, or in erecting monumental buildings for their rulers. There is evidence of the same centralized government, the same directing brain and organizing force that there is in primitive Babylonia.

Is it possible that two systems of engineering science,

so similar in their objects, their methods and their results, should have been invented independently in two different countries? There are scholars who answer in the negative. But the possibility cannot be denied, since an even more elaborate system of irrigation was invented in China without any suggestion, as far as we know, from outside. The geographical conditions of Babylonia and Egypt, moreover, resemble one another, and the question of draining the swamps and regulating the overflow of the rivers once raised, the answer to it seems fairly obvious. By itself, therefore, the fact that the cultures of ancient Babylonia and Egypt alike rested on a similar system of irrigation engineering would be no proof of their common origin.

In some respects the problem which the Babylonian engineers were called upon to solve was more difficult than that which faced the Egyptians. The Nile is fed by the rains and melting snows of Abyssinia and Central Africa, and its annual inundation takes place in the later summer months. The Euphrates and Tigris flow from the north, from the highlands ot Armenia, and are at their fullest in the spring. Their overflow accordingly comes just before the summer heats, when agriculture is difficult or impossible, whereas in Egypt the period of inundation ushers in the most favourable time of the year for the growth of the crops. What the Babylonian engineers had to do was not only to drain off the overflow, but also to store it for use at least six months later. With them it was a question of storage as well as of regulation.

Those then, who believe that the engineering sciences of the Babylonians and Egyptians were no independent inventions are bound to see in Babylonia their original home. It would have been here that the great problems were solved, the practical application of which to the needs of Egypt would have been a comparatively simple matter. On the chronological side there would be no difficulties in such a view. Old as was the civilization of Egypt, the excavations in Babylonia have made it clear that the civilization of Babylonia was at least equally old. At Nippur the American excavators claim to have found inscribed remains which reach back for nearly ten thousand years, and though the data upon which this calculation is based may be disputable, it is certain that the earliest monuments met with are of immense age. And it must be remembered that they belong to a time when the early pictorial writing had already passed into a cursive script, and the plain of Babylonia had been a land of cultivated fields for unnumbered generations.

But by itself, I repeat, the practical identity of engineering science in primeval Babylonia and Egypt is no proof that it had been learnt by the one from the other. If we are to fall back on the old belief which brought the civilized population of Egypt from the plain of Shinar, it must be for reasons which are supported by archæological facts. If such archæological facts exist, the parallel systems of irrigation engineering will be additional evidence; alone, they prove nothing.

At the outset we are met by a fact which personally I find it hard to explain away. The hieroglyphic script of Egypt has little in common with the primitive pictorial characters of Babylonia. Objects and ideas like "the sun," "man," "number one," will be represented by the same pictures or symbols all the world over, and consequently the fact that in both Babylonian and Egyptian writing the sun is denoted by a circle and the moon by a crescent is of no significance whatsoever. But when we turn to less obvious symbols there is comparatively little similarity between the two forms of script. The ideograph of "god," for example, is a star in Babylonia, a stone axe and its shaft in Egypt; "life" is represented by a flowering reed in the one case, by a knotted girdle in the other. It is true that Professor Hommel and others have pointed to a few coincidences like those between the Egyptian symbol for "foreign land" and the Babylonian ideograph of "country," or between the Egyptian and Babylonian signs for "city," "place," but such coincidences are rare.[1] As a rule, as soon as we leave the more obvious conventions of pictorial writing little or no connection can be traced between the pictorial characters of Egypt and those of Babylonia. As a whole the two graphic systems stand apart.

Nevertheless I am bound to add that it is only as a whole that they do so. With all the general unlikeness there is a curious similarity in a few—a very few—instances which it is difficult to interpret as merely the result of accident. The round circle with lines

---

[1] If, however, the Sumerian pictograph for "city" represents a tower on a mound, as seems to be the case, the identity in form of the Egyptian hieroglyph cannot be an accident, since both the tower and the artificial platform were essentially Babylonian. In the cursive cuneiform two separate pictographs have coalesced, one representing a seat, the other what appears to be a tower on a mound.

inside it which denotes "a city" in Egyptian might be explained from the circular villages which still characterize Central Africa; but then how is it that the ideograph for "place" in the pictorial script of Babylonia had precisely the same form? That the word for "country" should be denoted in the Babylonian script by the picture of three mountain peaks may be due to the fact that to the Babylonian "country" and "mountain" were the same; but such an explanation fails us in the case of the Egyptian hieroglyph of "foreign land," where the three peaks appear again, since the hieroglyph for "mountain" in Egyptian has but two. The picture of a seat, and a seat, too, of peculiar shape, represents "place" in Egyptian; in Babylonian the same picture represents "city," thus inverting the ideographic signification of the picture which in Egyptian and Babylonian has respectively the meanings of "city" and "place." Between the primitive Babylonian picture of a "ship" and the boats depicted in the prehistoric pottery of Egypt, again, the resemblance is very exact, and Professor Hommel has pointed out to me a curious likeness between the original form of the Babylonian ideograph for "a personal name" and the *ka*-sign with the Horus-hawk above it within which the names of the earliest Pharaohs are inscribed.[1]   Indeed the

---

[1] In Egyptian, however, the bird stands over a door, while in Babylonian it is over the two-legged stool on which two vases of offerings are set when it is used to denote the image of a god. The Sumerian pictograph for "(divine) lord" or "lady" (NIN) is the representation of a similar vase on a mat, and thus has the same form as the Egyptian *hotep*. The Egyptian *nefer*, "good," finds its exact counterpart in the Babylonian pictograph of "ornament" (ME-TE). The Babylonian "house," too, is given the same tower-like shape as the Egyptian (*āḥā*)

learned and ingenious Munich Professor has made out a list of even more striking coincidences, where the characters agree not only in sense but also in the phonetic values attached to them.[1]

Here, however, we trench on another question, the philological position of the Egyptian language. Egyptian scholars to-day are practically unanimous in believing it to belong, more or less remotely, to the Semitic family of speech. The Berlin school of Egyptologists, who under the guidance of Professor Erman have made Egyptian grammar a special subject of investigation, are largely responsible for the dominance of this belief. I ought to be the last person in the world to protest against it, seeing that I maintained it years ago when the patronage of the Berlin Egyptologists had not yet made it fashionable. At the same time I confess that I cannot follow the Berlin philologists to the extent to which they would have us go. For them the old Egyptian language is not related to the Semitic family of speech " more or less remotely," but very closely indeed. Indeed in their hands it becomes itself a Semitic language, and as a logical consequence the Egyptian script is metamorphosed into one of purely Semitic invention. But while admitting that Egyptian grammar is Semitic in the sense in which English grammar is Teutonic, the comparative philologist is bound to add that it contains much which cannot be reduced to a Semitic

---

[1] In a short Paper entitled *Lexicalische Belege zu meinen Vortrag über die sprachliche Stellung des Altægyptischen* (1895), in which he has attempted to draw up a list of phonetic equivalences between Egyptian and Sumerian. In this, however, I am unable to follow him, as his comparisons of Egyptian and Sumerian words are not convincing.

pattern. The structure, moreover, is not on the whole Semitic, neither is a large part of its vocabulary. And among the words in the lexicon which have Semitic affinities there are a good many which are better explained as the result of borrowing than as belonging to the original stratum of the language. In some cases they are demonstrably words which have been introduced into the Egyptian language at a late date ; in other cases it seems possible to regard them as loan-words from Semitic Babylonian which entered the language at a "pre-dynastic" epoch. Thus, *qemḵu* "the wheaten loaf" which was used for offerings, is the Hebrew *qemakh*, the Babylonian *qêmu*, and may have been brought into Eygpt along with the wheat which was first cultivated in Babylonia and still grows wild on the banks of the Euphrates. To what an early period the importation of the cereal must be referred is shown by its occurrence in the prehistoric graves of Upper Egypt.[1]

When all allowances are made, however, the fact remains that the Egyptian language as we know it was related to the Semitic family of speech. It stood to the latter as an elder sister, or rather as the sister of the parent-language which the existing Semitic dialects presuppose. It was not like the so-called Hamitic dialects of Eastern Africa, which are African languages Semitized, but it was itself of the same

---

[1] See de Morgan, *Recherches sur les Origines de l'Égypte*, pp. 94, 95. According to Schweinfurth, barley, which is also found in the prehistoric graves of Egypt, must originally have come from Babylonia like the wheat. *Qemḵu* is found in the Pyramid texts (Maspero, *Recueil de Travaux relatifs à la Philologie et à l'Archéologie égyptiennes et assyriennes*, v. p. 10). *Boti*, whence the Coptic *bôti* and the *battawa* or "durra cake" of modern Egyptian Arabic, was "durra," not "wheat."

stock as Hebrew or Semitic Babylonian. It represents, however, a form of language at an earlier stage of development than are any of those which we call Semitic, and it has, moreover, been largely influenced and modified by foreign languages, which we may term African. So extensive has this influence been that the Semitic element has been even more disguised in it than the Teutonic element is disguised in modern English. In leaving the soil of Asia the language of Egypt took upon it an African dress.

Now though language can prove but little as regards race, it can prove a great deal as regards history. A mixed language means a mixed history, and indicates an intimate contact between the populations who spoke the languages which are represented in it. Egyptian grammar would not have been Semitic if those who imposed it upon the natives of the Nile had not been of Semitic descent, or at all events had not come from a region where the language was Semitic. Nor would this grammar have been modified by foreign admixture if a part of those who learned to use it had not previously been accustomed to some other form of speech. And since we know of no Semitic languages in Africa which were not brought from Asia, we are justified in concluding that the Semitic element in the Egyptian language was of Asiatic origin.

But we can go yet a step further. Where two languages are brought into close contact, the general rule is that that of the stronger race prevails. The conqueror is less likely to learn the language of the conquered than the conquered are to learn the language of their masters. On the other hand, the negro slave

in America became English-speaking, whereas the
English emigrant wherever he goes preserves the
language of his fathers. It is only where a conquering
caste brings no women with it that it is likely to lose
its language.

When, therefore, we find that Old Egyptian is an
Africanized Semitic language, we have every right
to infer that it is because invaders brought it with
them from Asia who were Semites either by race or
by language. In other words, Egypt must have been
occupied in prehistoric days by a people who came
from the Semitic area in Asia.

The days were prehistoric, but of the invasion
itself history preserved a tradition. On the walls of
the temple of Edfu it is recounted how the followers
of Horus, the totem guide and patron deity of the
first kings of Upper Egypt, made their way across
the eastern desert to the banks of the Nile, and there,
with the help of their weapons of metal, subjugated
the older inhabitants of the valley. Battle after battle
was fought as the invaders slowly pushed their way
down the Nile to the Delta, establishing a forge and
a sanctuary of Horus on every spot where a victory
had been gained.[1] The story has come down to us
under a disguise of euhemeristic mythology, but the
tradition it embodies has been strikingly confirmed by
modern discovery. The "dynastic" Egyptians, the
Egyptians, that is to say, who founded the Egyptian
monarchy and to whom we owe the great monuments
of Egypt, were immigrants from the east.

The culture of these "dynastic" Egyptians was
built up on two solid foundations, the engineering

[1] See Maspero, *Études de Mythologie*, ii. pp. 313 *sqq.*

skill which made Egypt a land of agriculture, and a system of writing which made the organization of the government possible. The culture was at once agricultural and literary, and this alone marked it off from the culture of neolithic (or "prehistoric") Egypt, which belonged to the desert rather than to the banks and delta of the river, and which knew nothing of writing. Now we have seen that there was one other country in the world in which a similar form of culture had come into existence. In Babylonia too we have a civilization which has as its basis the training of rivers for the purpose of irrigation and the use of a pictorial script. The civilization of Babylonia was, it is true, Sumerian at its outset, but in time it became Semitic, and expressed itself in a Semitic tongue. It is difficult to avoid the conclusion that the Semitic-speaking people who brought the science of irrigation and the art of writing to the banks of the Nile came, like the wheat they cultivated, from the Babylonian plain.

There are two archæological facts connected with the early culture of "dynastic" Egypt which seem to me to prove at any rate some kind of intercourse with Babylonia. No building-stone exists in the Babylonian plain; it was therefore the natural home of the art of building in brick, and since every pebble was of value it was also the natural birthplace of the gem-cutter. Nowhere else could the use of clay as a writing material have suggested itself, or that of the inscribed stone cylinder which left its impression behind it when rolled over the clay. Wherever we have the clay tablet and the seal-cylinder we have evidence of Babylonian influence.

Now recent discoveries have shown that the culture of the early dynastic period of Egypt is distinguished from that of later times by the employment of clay and the stone seal-cylinder. Neither the one nor the other could have originated in the country itself, for Upper Egypt (where all authenticated discoveries of early seal-cylinders have been made) is a land of stone, and the river-silt, which is mixed with sand, is altogether unsuited for the purpose of writing. When the Egyptians of the Eighteenth dynasty corresponded in Babylonian cuneiform with their subjects and allies in Asia, the clay upon which they wrote was brought from a distance. Moreover, the stone seal-cylinder of the early dynasties is an exact reproduction of the early seal-cylinder of Babylonia. Substitute cuneiform characters for the hieroglyphs and there is practically no difference between them in many cases. It is difficult to believe that such an identity of form is the result of accident, more especially when we find that, as Egyptian civilization advanced, the seal-cylinder became less and less like its Babylonian original, and finally disappeared from use altogether. That is to say, as the culture of the people was further removed from its first starting-point, and therefore more national, an object which never had any natural basis in the physical conditions of the country grew more and more of an anomaly, and was eventually superseded, first by the "button-seal" and then by the scarab. I see no other explanation of this than that it was originally introduced from Babylonia, and maintained itself so long in an alien atmosphere only because it was bound up with a culture which had come from the same region of the world. The seal-cylinder of the early Egyptian dynasties seems to me, apart from everything else, to prove the existence of some kind of "prehistoric" intercourse between the civilizations of the Euphrates and the Nile. And in this intercourse the influences came from Babylonia to Egypt, not from Egypt to Babylonia.

The use of brick in early Egypt points in the same direction. While Babylonia was a land of clay, Upper Egypt was a land of stone, and it was as unnatural to invent the art of brick-making in the latter country as it was natural to do so in the former. To this day the Nubians build their cottages of stone ; so too do the Bedâwîn squatters on the east bank of the Nile ; it is only where the population is Egyptian and the influence of the old Egyptian civilization is still dominant that brick is employed. Under the Old Empire the Egyptian Pharaohs built even the temples of the gods of brick ; it was but gradually that the brick was superseded by stone. It was the same also in Assyria ; here too, in a land of stone, brick was at first the sole building material, and even the great brick platforms which the marshy soil of Babylonia had necessitated continued to be laid. But Assyrian culture was confessedly Babylonian in origin, and the brick edifice was therefore a characteristic of it. It was only by degrees that Assyrian architecture emancipated itself from its early traditions, and at first timidly, then more boldly, superseded the brick by stone. The example of Assyria throws light on that of Egypt, and as the Assyrian employment of brick was due to the Babylonian origin of its civilization, it is permissible to infer that the Egyptian employment of brick was also due to the same cause. Once more we may repeat that there was early intercourse between Egypt and Babylonia—the land of the brick-maker— and that in this intercourse the prevailing influences came from the east.

Such, then, is the conclusion to which the most recent research leads us. The "dynastic" Egyptians, the Egyptians of history, spoke a language which is related to those of the Semitic family; their first kingdoms, so far as we know, were in Upper Egypt, and tradition brought them across the eastern desert to the banks of the Nile. The culture which they possessed was characterized by Babylonian features, and was therefore due either wholly or in part to intercourse with Babylonia. The fact that the use of the seal-cylinder—which, by the way, bore the Semitic name of *khetem*—should have lingered in the valley of the Nile to the very beginnings of the Middle Empire, is an indication that the period of its introduction could not have been very remote. The earliest historical monuments which have been revealed to us by modern excavation may not, after all, be many centuries later than the time when the culture of Babylonia found its way to the Nile.

Indeed, there is a fact which indicates that this is the case, and that the literary culture of Babylonia had been imported into the valley of the Nile at a time when Egypt was divided into independent kingdoms. At an early epoch an ingenious system of official chronology had been invented in Babylonia. The years were named there after the chief events that had occurred in each of them, among these the accession or death of a king being naturally prominent. At the death of a king a list was drawn up of his regnal years, with their characteristic events, and such lists were from time to time combined into longer chronicles. The Babylonians were pre-eminently a commercial people, and for purposes of trade it was necessary that contracts and other legal documents should be dated accurately, and that in case of a dispute the date should be easily ascertained. Now an exactly similar system of dating had been adopted in Egypt before the age of the First historical dynasty. A pre-Menic monument dated in this way has been discovered at Hierakonpolis in Upper Egypt, and the same method of reckoning time is found on ivory tablets that have been disinterred at Abydos. The method lasted down to the age of the Fifth dynasty, since the Museum of Palermo contains the fragment of a stone from Heliopolis, on which the chronology of the Egyptian kings is given from Menes onward, each year being named after the event or events from which it had received its official title. The successive reigns are divided from one another as in the Babylonian lists, and the height of the Nile in each year is further added—a note which naturally is of Egyptian origin. It is, there-fore, interesting to observe that it is added as a note independent of the event which gave its name to the year. Nothing could prove more clearly the foreign origin of the whole system of chronology, since, had it been of native invention, the height of the Nile, on which the prosperity of the country depended, would have been the first event to be recorded. After the fall of the Old Empire this ancient Babylonian method of dating seems to have passed out of use like the Babylonian seal-cylinder ; at all events we find no further traces of it.   It was, in short, an exotic which never took kindly to Egyptian soil.

Did the "dynastic" Egyptians bring this method of dating with them, or did they borrow it after their settlement in Egypt ?   The second supposition is very difficult to entertain, for intimate trade relations between Babylonia and Upper (or Lower)[1] Egypt in the pre-Menic age appear to be out of the question, and are unsupported by any known facts.   And literary correspondence, such as was carried on in the time of the Eighteenth dynasty, seems equally out of the question.   How, then, did the Egyptians come to learn the peculiar Babylonian system of chronology unless the founders of the culture of which it formed a portion had originally brought it with them from the east ?

The same question is raised by the existence in early Egypt of an artistic *motif* which had its origin in Babylonia.   This is what is usually known as the

---

[1] I have put "Lower" between parentheses since it is very questionable whether this particular system of registering time was known in the Delta until it was introduced from Upper Egypt.   On the Palermo stone a list of the early kings of Lower Egypt is given, but without any dates, which make their appearance along with the kings of the First dynasty, who belonged to Upper Egypt.   It is interesting to observe that the ideograph for "year" is denoted in exactly the same way in both the Babylonian and the Egyptian hieroglyphs by the branch of a (palm) tree.   Such a curious symbol for the idea can hardly have been invented independently   Professor Hommel further draws attention to the fact that while the literal translation of a common ideographic mode of representing "year" in Babylonian is "name of heaven," that of the two syllables of the Egyptian word *renpet,* "year," would also be "name of heaven."

heraldic position of the figures of men and animals. An example of it is found on the famous "palette" of Nar-Buzau discovered by Mr. Quibell at Hierakonpolis,[1] where the hybrid monsters whose necks form the centre of the slate are heraldically arranged. In this case the design is known to be Babylonian, since M. Heuzey has pointed out a Babylonian sealcylinder on which the two monsters recur. Nar-Buzau is made the immediate predecessor of Menes by Professor Petrie on grounds to which every archæologist must assent; but an even better example of the heraldic design is met with on a great isolated rock of sandstone near El-Kab which was quarried in the time of the Old Empire. Here the ownership and opening of the quarry are denoted by an elaborate sculpture of the Pharaoh, who is duplicated, his two forms being figured as seated back to back, with a column between them, while the winged solar disk of Edfu, with the royal uræi on either side of the orb, spreads its wings above them. Each of the royal forms holds a sceptre, but that on the left has no head-dress, whereas that on the right wears a skullcap, above which is the solar orb with the uræus serpent issuing from it.[2] In front of the latter is an

[1] *Hierakonpolis*, part i. plate xxix. The name of the king is usually (but erroneously) written Nar-Mer.

[2] As the royal figures wear no crowns, they can hardly depict the king in his double office of king of Upper and Lower Egypt, and the duplication of the Pharaoh must consequently have a purely artistic origin. That this artistic origin is closely connected with the origin of the seal-cylinders is shown by the fact that the figures correspond with one of the most common designs on the latter, in which the *ka* of the person to whom the cylinder belonged is seated on a chair similar to that of the El-Kab king, an altar with offerings of bread being set before him.

altar consisting of a bowl on a stand, loaves of bread and a cup and jar of wine (with the customary handles for suspension) being engraved above the bowl along with a series of perpendicular lines which in this instance cannot (as has been suggested) represent the fringes of a mat. In front of the figure on the left is another altar, of different shape, the place of the bowl being taken by a flat top, above which are six upright lines and a flat cake. Precisely the same altar with the same objects above it are engraved on a broken seal-cylinder of ivory found by Dr. Reisner at Naga' ed-Dêr, which I understand from the discoverer to be of the age of the First dynasty. When, therefore, was it that the heraldic design in art was introduced into Egypt from its Babylonian birthplace? In any case it would seem to have been before the foundation of the united monarchy.

In Babylonia itself, as we have seen, tradition looked seaward, towards the Persian Gulf, for the elements of its civilization. At any rate the seaport of Eridu was the gateway through which the culture of Babylonia was believed to have passed. Here on the shores of the sea the culture-god of Sumer had his home; here trade sprang up, and the sailors and merchants of Eridu came into contact with men of other lands and other habits. Is it possible to discover a connection between Eridu and primeval Egypt?

I believe that it is, though in making the attempt we are of course treading upon precarious ground. There are certain curious coincidences, one of which, since it goes to the heart of Sumerian and Egyptian religion, is necessarily of considerable weight. But they are all, it must be remembered, more in the nature of indications and possibilities than of ascertained facts.

Eridu meant in Sumerian "the good city." Memphis (Men-nofer), "the good place," the name of the first capital of united Egypt, had the same signification. In the case of Eridu the name had something to do with the fact that the city was the seat of Ea, the god of beneficent spells and incantations, who had given the arts and sciences to man, and was ever ready to heal those that were sick. The son and vice-gerent of Ea, who carried his commands to earth and spent his time in curing diseases and raising "the dead to life," was Asari, "the prince," who was usually entitled Mulu-dugga, "the good" or "beneficent one." The character and attributes of Asari are thus the same as those of the Egyptian Osiris, who was also known as Ati, "the prince," and was commonly addressed as Un-nofer, "the good being." Unlike most of the Egyptian deities, Osiris had the same human form as Asari of Eridu, and the resemblance between the names of Asari and Osiris—Asar in Egyptian—is rendered more striking by the remarkable fact that they are both represented by two ideographs or hieroglyphs of precisely the same shape and signification.[1] It does not appear possible to ascribe such a threefold identity to mere coincidence. And the theory of coincidence becomes still more improbable when we remember that while the story of Osiris centres in his death and resurrection, one of the chief offices of the Sumerian Asari was to

[1] The eye and the ideograph of city or place. Since the eye here has the phonetic value of *eri* or *ari*, the ideograph of "city," which is *eri* in Sumerian, must have the Egyptian value of *as*.

"raise the dead to life." Nowhere else in Babylonian literature, whether Sumerian or Semitic, do we find any reference to a resurrection ; the Semitic Babylonians, indeed, did not look forward to a future life at all, or if they did, it was to a shadowy existence in a subterranean land of darkness "where all things are forgotten." It is only in connection with Asari that we hear of a possibility that the dead may live again.

Other resemblances between the theologies of Eridu and primitive Egypt have been pointed out. Professor Hommel believes that in the Egyptian deity Nun, the heavenly ocean, we must see a Sumerian god Nun, who also represented the celestial abyss. However this may be, an old formula, torn from its context, which has been introduced into the Pyramid texts of the Pharaoh Pepi I., takes us back not only to the cosmology of Eridu but to the literary form in which it had been expressed. Pepi, it is said, "was born of his father Tum. At that time the heaven was not, the earth was not, men did not exist, the gods were not born, there was no death." The words are almost a repetition of those with which the Babylonian epic of the creation begins : "At that time the heaven above was not known by name, the earth beneath was not named . . . at that time the gods had not appeared, any one of them"; and they are also a distant echo of the commencement of the cosmological legend of Sumerian Eridu : "At that time no holy house, no house of the gods in a holy place had been built, no reed had grown, no tree had been planted." [1]

The testimony of philological archæology, if I may

---

[1] See my *Religions of Ancient Egypt and Babylonia*, p. 238.

use such a term, is supplemented by that of archæological discovery. Sumerian Babylonia and early dynastic Egypt are alike characterized by vases of hard stone, many of which have the same forms. Examples of some of them will be found in de Morgan's *Recherches sur les Origines de l'Égypte*, ii. p. 257, where Jéquier observes that analogues to the Egyptian vases have been disinterred by de Sarzec at Tello in Southern Babylonia, "the shape and execution of which are exactly like" those discovered in Egypt, "the only difference being that the one are ornamented with hieroglyphics, and the others with a cuneiform inscription; apart from this they are identical in make." The most remarkable instance of identity, however, is the design on the palette of the pre-Menic Pharaoh Nar-Buzau to which attention was first called by Professor Heuzey.[1] On this we have a representation of two lions set face to face in the Babylonian fashion, and with long serpentine necks which are interlaced so as to enclose a circle. Precisely the same representation is met with on an early Babylonian seal-cylinder from Tello.

Years ago I noticed the general likeness presented by the seated statues of Tello to those of the Third Egyptian dynasty,[2] and suggested that both belonged to the same school of sculpture. A little earlier Professor Flinders Petrie had demonstrated that the

[1] *Comptes rendus de l'Académie des Inscriptions et Belles Lettres*, 4 Sér., 1899, xxvii. pp. 60–67 ; see *Hierakonpolis*, part ii. plate xxviii. In the *Revue d'Assyriologie*, v. pp. 29–32, Heuzey has lately drawn attention to the resemblance between the early Egyptian and Babylonian bowls of calcite or Egyptian alabaster.

[2] *Lectures on the Religion of the Ancient Babylonians*, 1887, p. 33.

standard of measurement marked upon the plan of the city which one of the Tello figures holds in his lap is the same as the standard of measurement of the Egyptian pyramid-builders, the cubit, namely, of 20·63, which is quite different from the later Assyro-Babylonian cubit of 21·6.[1] Still more convincing, perhaps, is the Babylonian division of the year into twelve months of thirty days each, which was already known in Egypt in the age of the early dynasties. The Babylonian week of five and ten days reappears in the Egyptian week of ten days, while the division of the day into twelve "double hours," six belonging to the day and six to the night, has its counterpart in the Egyptian day of twenty-four hours, twelve of which were reckoned to the day and the other twelve to the night. Since a list of the thirty-six decans or zodiacal stars has recently been found on a coffin of the time of the Twelfth Dynasty[2] it is possible that this distinctively Babylonian invention may also go back to the age of the first Egyptian dynasties. At all events one of the chief stars in the Pyramid texts is "the Bull of heaven," a translation of the Sumerian Gudi-bir, or "Bull of Light," the name given to the planet Jupiter in its relation to the ecliptic. In primitive Babylonian astronomy the zodiacal sign of the Bull ushered in the year.

It may be that some of these evidences of Babylonian influence are referable to contact between Babylonia and Egypt in the age that immediately preceded the foundation of the united Egyptian

---

[1] *Nature*, August 9, 1883, p. 341.
[2] Daressy, " Le Cercueil d'Emsaht," in the *Annales du Service des Antiquités de l'Égypte*, 1899, i. pp. 79–90.

monarchy rather than to that still earlier age when the "dynastic" settlers first settled in the valley of the Nile. But at present we do not know how such a contact could have taken place. Upper Egypt and not the Delta was the seat of the first Pharaohs with their Horus-hawk totem, and at the remote period when the future civilization of the country was being developed under their fostering care it is difficult to believe that Babylonian soldiers or traders had made their way to the shores of the Mediterranean, much less to the deserts of the Sayyîd. For the present, at all events, where we have clear proof of the dependence of early Egyptian culture upon that of the Babylonians we have no alternative but to ascribe it to the Semitic emigrants or invaders to whom the historical civilization of Egypt was primarily due.[1]

This civilization, like that of Babylonia, implied a

[1] I have called Upper Egypt the seat of the first Pharaohs, not only because the earliest dynastic monuments we possess come from thence, but also because it was of Upper Egypt and its ruling caste that the hawk-god Horus was the guardian deity. From Upper Egypt he was carried to Lower Egypt and its nomes, presumably through conquest, as is monumentally attested by the "palette" of Nar-Buzau discovered at Hierakonpolis (Capart, *Débuts de l'Art en Égypte*, p. 236). So, too, the anthropomorphic Osiris—the duplicate of Anhur—made his way from the south to the north. That Southern Arabia should have been the connecting-link between Babylonia and Egypt was the result of its being the source of the incense which was imported for religious use into both countries alike at the very beginning of their histories. That this foreign product should have been considered an indispensable adjunct of the religions of the two civilizations is one of the best proofs we have of their connection with one another. Dr. Schweinfurth has shown that the sacred trees of Egypt—the sycamore and the persea—which needed artificial cultivation for their preservation there, came from Southern Arabia, where he found them growing wild under the names of *Khanes, Burra and Lebakh* (*Verhandlungen der Gesellschaft für Erdkünde zu Berlin*, July 1889, No. 7).

knowledge of metal. It was a civilization of the copper age, and thus stood in sharp contrast to the neolithic culture, such as it was, of " prehistoric " Egypt. Egyptian tradition, it is true, believed that the metal weapons with which the followers of Horus had overcome the stone-defended natives of the country were of iron, but this was because the compilers of the story in its existing form projected the knowledge and usages of their own time back into the past. There is incontrovertible proof that in Egypt, as in Europe, the ages of copper and bronze preceded that of iron. But the tradition was doubtless right in laying stress upon the fact that the invaders were forgers and blacksmiths. It would have been by reason of the superiority of their arms that they succeeded in subduing the valley of the Nile and reducing its inhabitants to serfdom. They were, too, "the followers of Horus," under the leadership of a single prince who was himself a Horus, that is to say, an incarnate god. Here, again, we find ourselves in the presence of a conception and doctrine of Semitic Babylonia. There, too, as we have seen, the kings were incarnate gods, not only the sons of a divinity, but themselves divine. In Egypt, apart from the Osirian circle, the gods were not men, but animals, and so deeply rooted was this beast-worship in the hearts of the indigenous population that even the " dynastic " civilization, with all its unifying and absorbing power, never succeeded in doing more than in uniting the head of the beast with the body of the man. Even the human Pharaoh was forced to picture himself as a hawk. In Semitic Babylonia on the other hand, as we have seen, the deification of the king flowed naturally from the anthropomorphic conception of the deity ; where man was made in the image of God, it was easy to see in him a god on earth. Like the use of copper, therefore, the deification of the king which characterized dynastic Egypt points back to Babylonia.

It must not be supposed, however, that because certain elements and leading characteristics in the civilization of historical Egypt indicate that the Semitic-speaking race to whom it was mainly due came originally from Babylonia, there are no elements in it which can be derived from elsewhere. On the contrary, there is much that is native to Egypt itself. Even the script shows but comparatively few traces of a Babylonian origin. If the "dynastic" Egyptians came from Babylonia, they must have very considerably modified and developed the seeds of culture which they brought with them. And in Egypt they found a neolithic culture which had already made considerable progress. The indigenous population possessed the same artistic sense as the palæolithic European of the Solutrian and Magdalenian epochs, with whom perhaps it was contemporaneous, and under the direction of its dynastic conquerors this sense was trained and educated until the Egyptians of history became one of the most artistic peoples of the old world.

But it is noticeable that throughout the historical period whenever the civilizations of Egypt and Babylonia came into contact, it was Egypt that was influenced rather than Asia. The tradition of the earliest ages was thus carried on ; the stream of influence flowed from the east, and Herodotus was justified in assigning Egypt to Asia rather than to Africa. It was, in fact, Asia with an African colouring. In the days of the Eighteenth dynasty, when Egypt for the first and last time possessed an Asiatic empire, the eastern influence is very marked. The script itself became Babylonian, the correspondence of the Government with its own officials in Canaan was conducted in the Babylonian language and the Babylonian syllabary, and there are indications that even the official memoranda of the campaigns of Thothmes III. were drawn up in cuneiform characters. The clay tablets of Babylonia were imitated in Upper Egypt, where hieroglyphic and hieratic characters were somewhat awkwardly impressed upon them, and the language was filled with Semitic loan-words. The fashionable author of the age of the Nineteenth dynasty interlarded his style not only with Semitic words, but even with Semitic phrases. It is true that the Semitic words and phrases are Canaanite; but Canaan had long been a province of Babylonia, and it was because it was permeated with Babylonian culture and used the Babylonian script, that the foreign words and phrases were introduced into the literary language of Egypt.

On the other hand, so far as we can judge, there was no reflex action of Egypt upon Babylonia. The seal-cylinder was never superseded there by the scarab; indeed the only scarabs yet found in the Mesopotamian region are memorials of the Egyptian conquests of the Eighteenth dynasty. Neither the hieroglyphs nor the hieratic of Egypt made their way eastward into Asia, a fact which is somewhat remarkable when we remember over how wide an area the more complicated cuneiform spread. It was Europe that was affected by Egypt rather than Asia. Before Egypt laid claim to Palestine, Babylonian culture had already taken too firm a hold of Western Asia to be dislodged, and in Babylonia itself Egyptian influences are hard to find. In the age of Khammu-rabi, we meet with a few proper names which may contain the name of the Sun-god Ra, as well as with the name of Anupum or Anubis on a stone cylinder, and the hieroglyphic character *nefer*, "good," is affixed to a legal document.[1] But this merely proves that in a period when the Babylonian Empire reached to the confines of Egypt, there were Egyptians settled in Babylon for the purpose of trade. A more curious example of possible Egyptian influence is one to which I have drawn attention in my lectures on the *Religions of Ancient Egypt and Babylonia*.[2] Thoth, the Egyptian god of literature, was accompanied by four apes, who sang hymns to the rising and setting sun. Travellers have described the dancing and screaming of troops of apes at daybreak when the sun first lights up the earth, and the origin of these companions of Thoth has been cleared up by an inscription in a tomb at Assuan. Here we learn that in the age of the Old Empire, expeditions were sent by the Pharaohs into the Sudan—the home of the apes of Thoth—in order to bring back from "the land of the gods" Danga

[1] In the possession of Lord Amherst of Hackney. On an early Babylonian seal-cylinder, bought by Dr. Scheil at Mossul and figured in the *Recueil de Travaux relatifs à la Philologie et à l'Archéologie égyptiennes et assyriennes*, xix. 1, 2, No. 7 of the plate, we have : "Ili-su-bani son of Aminanum, servant of the gods Bel and Anupum." Aminanum may be a Semitized form of the Egyptian Ameni.

[2] Pp. 133, 139 485.

dwarfs who could "dance the dances of the gods." In the eyes of the Egyptians, it would seem, there was little difference between the ape and the Danga dwarf; the one was a dwarf-like ape, the other an ape-like man. But they alone could perform correctly the dances that were held in honour of certain gods, and which are already depicted on the prehistoric vases of Egypt.[1] Closely allied to the Danga dwarfs and the apes of Thoth are the Khnumu or Patæki of Memphis, the followers of Ptah, who were also dwarfs with bowed legs. Now dwarfs of precisely the same form are found on early Babylonian seal-cylinders where they are associated sometimes with the goddess Istar, sometimes with an ape and the god Sin.[2] The Babylonian name of the dwarf was the Sumerian Nu-gidda, an indication that his association with the deity went back to Sumerian times. We may conclude that, like the Danga dwarf of Egypt, he, too, performed dances in honour of the gods.

The extraordinary resemblance of form between the Egyptian and Babylonian sacred dwarfs, as represented in art, raises the question whether the Babylonian dwarf was not an importation from Egypt, since the ape with which he was confounded was a native of the Sudan. This was the view to which I was long inclined, but there are certain considerations which make it difficult to be accepted.

---

[1] De Morgan, *Recherches sur les Origines de l'Égypte*, p. 65.

[2] Scheil, *Recueil de Travaux relatifs à la Philologie et à l'Archéologie égyptiennes et assyriennes*, xix. pp. 50, 54 ; Sayce, *Religions of Ancient Egypt and Babylonia*, p. 485. The dwarf is represented as dancing before the god Sin on an early Babylonian seal-cylinder published by Scheil in the *Recueil*, xix. 1, 2, No. 16 of the plate.

The Khnumu of Memphis were not the only dwarfs who were represented by the Egyptian artists. Still better known was Bes, who became a special favourite in the Roman period, when he was made a sort of patron of childbirth. But Bes, it was remembered, had come to Egypt from the southern lands of Somali and Arabia, like the goddess Hathor or the god Horus. Hathor is, I believe, the Babylonian Istar, who has passed to Egypt through her South Arabian name of Athtar; however this may be, Ptah of Memphis, whose followers were the Khnumu dwarfs, bears a Semitic name, and must therefore be of Semitic derivation. He belongs, that is to say, to the Egyptians of the dynastic stock, and is accordingly one of the few Egyptian divinities who is depicted in human form. On the other hand, the Sumerian dwarf Nu-gidda is the companion of Istar.

On the Egyptian side, therefore, the dwarfs of Ptah are associated with a god who has come from Asia, while the dwarf Bes was confessedly of foreign extraction. On the Babylonian side the dwarf Nu-gidda was the associate of Istar, the counterpart of Hathor, and of Sin, the Moon-god, who was adopted by the people of Southern Arabia, and whose name was carried as far as Mount Sinai on the borders of Egypt. All this suggests that the sacred dwarf came to the valley of the Nile from Babylonia and Arabia like the name of Ptah, the creator of the world. In this case it would have come with the dynastic Egyptians before the age of history begins.

But, on the other hand, there is the ape, and the ape is figured along with the dwarf on the Babylonian seals. It is true that the ape is equally foreign to

I

Egypt and Babylonia, but the Sudan is nearer Egypt than Southern Arabia is to Babylonia. The actual date and path of migration, therefore, of the sacred dwarf must be left undecided. Whether he was brought to Egypt at the dawn of history, or whether he travelled to Babylonia in the historical age remains doubtful. All we can be sure of is that the sacred dwarfs of Babylonia and Egypt were originally one and the same, and that they testify to an intercourse between the two countries of which all literary record has been lost.[1]

The same verdict must be given in the case of another point, not only of resemblance, but of identity, between ancient Egypt and Babylonia. This is the shadûf or contrivance for drawing water from a falling river for the sake of irrigation. The shadûf, which is still used in Upper Egypt, can be traced back pictorially to the time of the Eighteenth dynasty, but the basin system of irrigation with which it was connected was already of immemorial antiquity. It is a simple yet most effective invention, and on that account perhaps the less likely to have been independently invented, for it is always the obvious which remains longest unnoticed. In the modern shadûf a long pole is laid across a beam which is supported at either end upon other poles or on pillars of brick or mud; it is kept in place by thongs and is heavily weighted at one end, while at the other end a bucket or skin is attached to it by means of a rope. The shadûf of the

---

[1] It is worth notice that the dwarf-god Bes, who is called "God of Punt" in inscriptions of the Ptolemaic age, appears on Arab coins of the Roman period (Schweinfurth, *Verhandlungen der Gesellschaft für Erdkunde* 1889, No. 7).

Eighteenth dynasty was supported sometimes, as to-day, on a cross-beam, sometimes on a column of mud, and the bucket was of triangular form with two handles to which the rope was tied. Representations of it from Theban tombs will be found in Maspero's *Dawn of Civilization*, p. 764, and Sir Gardner Wilkinson's *Ancient Egyptians*, plates 38 and 356. Precisely the same machine is represented on a bas-relief found by Layard in the palace of Kûyunjik at Nineveh,[1] the only difference being that the shadûf-worker stands upon a platform of brick instead of on the bank itself, and that the pillar upon which the pole is supported seems to be built of bricks rather than of mud. The machine, however, is identical in both its Egyptian and its Assyrian form. That the bas-relief should have been found in Assyria and not in Babylonia is a mere accident. Like almost every-thing else in Assyrian culture, the invention was of Babylonian origin, and, in fact, formed part of the system of irrigation which made the plain of Babylonia habitable. Herodotus, who calls the machine a κηλωνεῖον, describes it as being used as in Egypt, and for the same reason, since the river did not rise to the actual level of the cultivated ground, which, like that of Egypt, was divided into a number of basins.[2]

The palace of Kûyunjik belongs to the last age of Assyrian history. But the shadûf in Babylonia went back to the Sumerian period, as we know from the references to it in the lexical tablets. It was called *dulâtum* in Semitic Babylonian, the pole or poles being *kakritum*, and the bucket *zirqu* or *zirqatum*

---

[1] Layard, *Monuments of Nineveh*, Second Series, pl. 15.
[2] Herodotus, i. 193.

(Sumerian *sû*),[1] and an old Sumerian collection of agricultural precepts describes how the irrigator "fixes up the shadûf, hangs up the bucket and draws water."[2] The "irrigator" was naturally an important personage in early Babylonia, and legend averred that the famous Sargon of Akkad, the founder of the first Semitic Empire, had been rescued as a child from a watery grave, and brought up by one. In both Babylonia and Egypt the shadûf was closely associated with a system of irrigation which went back to the dawn of their several histories.

What explanation must we give of its identity in the two countries? There are three possibilities. In the first place, it may have been invented independently on the banks of both the Euphrates and the Nile. Similar conditions tend to produce similar results. But against this is the fact that the shadûf was not the only kind of irrigating machine that was suggested by the nature of the two rivers and the lands through which they flowed. In modern Egypt, besides the shadûf there are the *saqia*, or water-wheel, and an irrigating contrivance which is in use in the Delta. The water-wheel, we know, was a Babylonian invention which was imported into Egypt in comparatively recent times ; the irrigating contrivance of the Delta, which consists of a bucket suspended on a rope swung by two men who stand facing each other, is a primitive instrument which might have been invented anywhere. Its survival is due to the fact that in the flat marshes of the Delta, the shadûf, though saving labour, is not

---

[1] The rope appears to have been *makutum;* see *W. A. I.* v. 26, 61.
[2] K. 56, ii. 14.

necessary, and it therefore continued to be employed there after the shadûf was known. But this implies that the shadûf was not the oldest instrument for raising the water of the Nile.

Then there is the second possibility that the shadûf was borrowed by Egypt from Babylonia or by Babylonia from Egypt in historical times. In Babylonia, however, we can trace its history back to the Sumerian epoch, and in both countries it was intimately connected with a system of irrigation the origin of which must be sought in the prehistoric age, and which was probably carried from the valley of the Euphrates to that of the Nile. There remains the third possibility that it came to Egypt along with the system of irrigation itself.

It is always easier to ask questions than to answer them, in archæology as in other things. There are many details connected with the early relationship between the civilizations of Babylonia and Egypt which must be left to future research to discover. But of that relationship there can now be little question in the minds of those who are accustomed to deal with inductive evidence. There was intercourse in the prehistoric age between the two countries, and the civilizing influences, like the wheat and the language, came from the lands which bordered on the Euphrates. Civilized man made his way from the east, and dwelt in primeval days " in the land of Shinar."[1]

[1] For other evidences of contact between primitive Babylonia and early Egypt, see Heuzey in the *Revue d'Assyriologie*, 1899, v. 2, pp. 53–6. He there enumerates (1) the resemblance between the stone mace-heads of the two countries in "prehistoric times," as well as between the flat dishes of veined and ribboned onyx marble, hollowed and rounded by the hand ; (2)

between the lion-heads of stone, the onyx stone of one of which is stated in an inscription to have come from Magan ; (3) the extraordinary likeness in the delineation of animal forms, which extends to conventional details "like the two concentric curves artificially arranged so as to allow the two corners of the profile to be visible at the same time " ; (4) the use of a razor and the custom of completely shaving the face, and even the skull ; and (5) the ceremonial form of libation by means of a vase of peculiar shape, with a long curved spout and without a handle. This libation vase was practically the same in both countries, in spite of its peculiar and somewhat complicated form. Of later introduction into Egypt was the inscribed cone of terra-cotta, which was of early Babylonian origin, but is not met with in Egypt before the age of the Twelfth dynasty. At any rate, the first specimens of it hitherto found there were discovered by myself at Ed-Dêr, opposite Esna, in 1905 (*Annales du Service des Antiquités de l'Égypt*, 1905, pp. 164–5).

CHAPTER V

BABYLONIA AND PALESTINE

A VERY few years ago Palestine was still archæologically an unknown land. Its history subsequent to the Israelitish conquest could be gathered from the Old Testament, and Egyptian papyri of the age of the Nineteenth dynasty had told us something about its condition immediately prior to that event. Thanks to the Palestine Exploration Fund, the country had been carefully surveyed, and the monuments still existing on its surface had been noted and registered. But the earlier history of the people, their races and origin, their social and religious life, and their relation to the rest of the world, were still a blank. Of the Canaan invaded by the children of Israel we knew nothing from an archæological point of view, and very little even of the Palestine that was governed by Israelitish judges and Jewish kings.

The veil has at last been lifted which so long lay over the face of Palestine. Cuneiform texts have come to clear up its civil history, while the spade of the excavator has supplemented their evidence on the more purely archæological side. The history of Palestine can now be followed back not only into the neolithic, but even into the palæolithic age, and the source and character of Canaanite civilization have been in large measure revealed to us.

First and foremost among the materials which have made this possible are the cuneiform tablets of Tel el-Amarna in Upper Egypt, which were discovered in 1887. Tel el-Amarna, about midway between Minia and Assiut, is the site of a city which sprang, like a meteor, into a brief but glorious existence under the so-called "heretic king" Amon-hotep IV. about B.C. 1400. Amon-hotep, under the guidance of his mother, had endeavoured to suppress the old state religion of Egypt, and to substitute for it a pantheistic mono-theism. In spite of persecution, however, the adherents of the old faith proved too strong for the king; he was forced to leave Thebes, the capital of his fathers, and to build a new capital further north, where he changed his name to that of Khu-n-Aten, and called artists from the islands of the Mediterranean to adorn his palace. When moving from Thebes he naturally transferred to the new seat of government both the Foreign Office and its records in so far as they covered the reign of his father Amon-hotep III. and his own. For reasons unknown to us they do not extend further back.

They were all in the cuneiform script, and for the most part in the Babylonian language. The fact came upon the historian with a shock of surprise, and had far-reaching consequences, historical as well as archæological. In the first place, they proved what had already been suspected, that under the Eighteenth dynasty Egypt possessed an Asiatic empire which stretched to the banks of the Euphrates. Then, secondly, they showed that Western Asia was at the

time intersected by high-roads along which merchants
and couriers were constantly passing, and an active
literary correspondence was carried on. Thirdly—
and this was the greatest surprise of all—they made it
clear that this correspondence was in the script and
language of Babylonia, and that it was shared in by
writers of various nationalities and languages, of all
classes of society and of both sexes. The Hittite and
Cappadocian kings wrote to the Pharaoh in cuneiform
characters, just as did the kings of Babylonia and
Assyria. Arab shêkhs and Hittite condottieri joined
in the correspondence, and politically-minded ladies
did the same. Even the Egyptian Government was
compelled to suppress all feelings of national vanity,
and to conduct the whole of its correspondence with
its own governors and vassals in Palestine or Syria in
the foreign language and syllabary. There is no trace
anywhere of the use of either the Egyptian language
or the Egyptian mode of writing.

From these facts other facts follow. The age of
the Eighteenth Egyptian dynasty must have been
quite as literary as the age of our own eighteenth
century, and international correspondence must have
been quite as easy, if not easier. Education, moreover, must have been very widely spread; all the
civilized world was writing and reading; and the system
of writing was a most complicated one, demanding
years of study and memory. In spite of this it was
known not only to a professional class of scribes and
the officials of the Government, but also to the shêkhs
of petty Canaanitish towns and even to Bedâwîn
chiefs. And along with the system of writing went
a knowledge of the foreign language of Babylonia—

the French of Western Asia—including some slight acquaintance with the extinct language of the Sumerians. All this presupposes libraries and archive-chambers where books and dispatches could be stored, as well as schools where the Babylonian script and language could be taught and learned.

Such libraries and schools had existed in Babylonia from a very early age. Every great city had its library, every great temple its muniment-room. Here the clay books were numbered and arranged on shelves, catalogues being provided which gave their titles. The system under which the longer literary or semi-scientific works were arranged and catalogued was at once ingenious and complete. By the side of the library was naturally the school. Here every effort was made to facilitate the progress of the scholars, more especially in the study of the Sumerian language and texts. The characters of the syllabary were classified and named; comparative grammars, dictionaries and reading-books of Sumerian and Semitic Babylonian were compiled, lists of Semitic synonyms were drawn up, explanatory commentaries were written on older works, and interlinear transla-tions provided for the Sumerian texts. But with all this the cuneiform system of writing must have been hard even for the native Babylonian to learn, and in the case of the foreigner its difficulties were multiplied. It may be doubted whether the average boy of to-day, who finds the spelling of his own English almost too much for him, would have had the memory and patience to learn the cuneiform characters. Even in Sumerian times the difficulty of the task was realized, for there is a Sumerian proverb that " he who would excel in the school of the scribes must rise with the dawn." [1] It says much for the educational zeal of the Oriental world in the century before the Exodus that it was just this difficult and complicated script which it chose as its medium for correspondence.

The fact, however, points unmistakably to its cause. The reason why the Babylonian language and syllabary were thus in use throughout Western Asia, and why even the Egyptian Government was obliged to employ them in its communications with its Asiatic subjects, can only have been because Babylonian culture was too deeply rooted there to be superseded by any other. Before Egypt appeared upon the scene under the conquerors of the Eighteenth dynasty, Western Asia, as far as the Mediterranean, must have been for centuries under the direct influence and domination of Babylonia. I say domination as well as influence, for in the ancient East military conquest was needed to enforce an alien language and literature, theology and system of law upon another people. And even military conquest was not always sufficient, as witness the Assyrian and Persian conquests of Egypt, or the Roman conquest of Syria.

We now have monumental testimony that such domination there actually was. As far back as B.C. 3800, Sargon of Akkad had founded a Semitic empire which had its centre in Babylon, and which stretched across Asia to the shores of the Mediterranean. We learn from his annals that three campaigns were needed to subdue " the land of the Amorites," as

[1] *Recueil de Travaux*, etc., xvi. p. 190.

Syria and Palestine were called, and that at last, after three years of warfare, all the coast-lands of "the sea of the setting sun" acknowledged his sway. He set up an image of himself on the Syrian coast in commemoration of his victories, and moulded his conquests "into one" great empire. His son and successor, Naram-Sin, extended his conquests into the Sinaitic peninsula, and a seal-cylinder, on which he is adored as a god, has been found in Cyprus. But Sargon was a patron of literature as well as a conqueror ; his court was filled with learned men, and one of the standard works of Babylonian literature is said to have been compiled during his reign. The extension of Babylonian rule, therefore, to Western Asia meant the extension of Babylonian civilization, an integral part of which was its script.

Here, then, is an explanation of the archæological fact that the graves of the copper and early bronze age in Cyprus, which mark the beginning of civilization in the country, contain numerous seal-cylinders made in imitation of those of Babylonia.[1] Examples of the seal-cylinders from which they were copied have also been discovered there. Among them is the cylinder on which Naram-Sin is adored as a god, another is an extremely fine specimen of the style that was current in the age of Sargon of Akkad.[2] Along with the seal-cylinder it is probable that the

[1] In the later bronze or "Mykenæan" age the seal-cylinders are of a different type, and are engraved on a black artificial paste resembling hæmatite (Myres and Ohnefalsch-Richter, *Catalogue of the Cyprus Museum*, p. 32).

[2] Sayce, *Transactions of the Society of Biblical Archæology*, 1877, v. part ii. ; Bezold, *Zeitschrift für Keilinschrift*, 1885, pp. 191–3.

clay tablet was also introduced to the people of the West. Though the clay tablets found by Dr. Evans and others in Krete may not go back to so remote a date, the linear Kretan characters belong to the same system of writing as the Cypriote syllabary, and an inscription in the letters of this syllabary on a seal-cylinder from the early copper-age cemetery of Paraskevi near Nikosia has recently been published by myself.[1] We may infer that the prototypes of the tablets of Knossos or Phæstos once existed in Cyprus and Syria, though in the damp climate of the Mediterranean the unbaked clay of which they were made has long since returned to its original dust.

A few centuries after the age of Sargon of Akkad we find Gudea, a Sumerian prince in Southern Babylonia, bringing limestone from "the land of the Amorites," blocks of alabaster from the Lebanon, and beams of cedar from Mount Amanus, for his buildings in the city of Lagas. Gold-dust and acacia wood were at the same time imported from the "salt" desert which lay between Palestine and Egypt, and stones from the mountains of the Taurus, to the north-east of the Gulf of Antioch, were floated down the Euphrates on rafts.[2] At a later date we hear of the kings of the Babylonian dynasty which had its capital at Ur, conducting military expeditions to the district of the Lebanon.

[1] *Proceedings of the Society of Biblical Archæology*, November 1905, plate No. 11.

[2] A cadastral survey, which was drawn up at this period under Uru-malik, or Urimelech, "the governor of the land of the Amorites," would, if perfect, have given us an interesting description of Syria and Palestine in the third millennium before our era ; see Thureau Dangin in the *Revue Sémitique*, Avril 1897.

About B.C. 2300 Northern Babylonia was occupied by a dynasty of kings, whose names show that they belonged to the Western division of the Semitic family. The language of Canaan—better known to us as Hebrew—and that of Southern and North-eastern Arabia, were at the time substantially one and the same, and as the same deities were worshipped and the same ancestors were claimed throughout this portion of the Semitic world, Assyriologists are not agreed as to whether the dynasty in question should be regarded as coming from Canaan or from Southern Arabia. The Babylonians themselves called the names Amorite, so it is possible that they would have pronounced the kings to have been Amorite also. The point, however, is of little moment ; the fact remains that Northern Babylonia passed under the rule of sovereigns who belonged to the Western and not to the Babylonian branch of the Semitic race, and who made Babylon their capital. The contract tablets and other legal documents of this period show that Babylonia was at the time full of Amorite, that is Canaanite, settlers, most of whom had come there for the sake of trade. At Sippara there was a district called "the field of the Amorites," over which, therefore, they must have had full legal rights. Indeed, it would seem that in the eyes of the law the Amorite settlers were on a complete footing of equality with the natives of the country.

This fact, so little in harmony with our ordinary idea of the exclusiveness of the ancient East, is largely explained by the further fact that Canaan and Syria were now acknowledged portions of the Babylonian Empire. When Babylonia was conquered

by the Elamites, and the West Semitic king of
Babylon allowed to retain his crown as an Elamite
vassal, his claim to rule over "the land of the
Amorites" passed naturally to his suzerain. Accordingly we find Chedor-laomer of Elam in the Book of
Genesis marching to Canaan to put down a local
rebellion there, while Eri-Aku, or Arioch, of Larsa,
at the same date describes an Elamite prince as
"governor of the land of the Amorites." When
Khammu-rabi, or Amraphel, the king of Babylon,
at last succeeded in shaking off the Elamite yoke
and making himself monarch of a free and united
Babylonia, "the land of the Amorites" followed the
fortunes of Babylonia as a matter of course. On a
monument discovered at Diarbekir, in Northern
Mesopotamia, the only title taken by the Babylonian
sovereign is that of "king of the land of the Amorites." And the same title is borne by one at least of
his successors in the dynasty.

For more than two thousand years, therefore,
Western Asia was more or less closely attached to
Babylonia. At times it was as much a part of the
dominions of the Babylonian king as the cities of
Babylonia itself, and it is consequently not surprising
that it should have become thoroughly interpenetrated
with Babylonian culture. There was an excellent
postal service connecting Canaan with Babylonia
which went back to the days of Naram-Sin, and some
of the clay *bullæ* which served as stamps for the
official correspondence at that period are now in the
Museum of the Louvre.[1] On the other hand, a clay
docket has been found in the Lebanon, dated in the

[1] See Heuzey, in the *Revue d'Assyriologie*, 1897, pp. 1-12.

reign of the son of Khammu-rabi, which contains one of the notices sent by the Babylonian Government to its officials at the beginning of each year, in order that they might know what was its official title and date.[1]

When this close connection between Babylonia and its Syrian provinces was broken off we do not as yet know. Perhaps it did not take place until the conquest of Babylonia by a horde of half-civilized mountaineers from Elam about B.C. 1800. At any rate, from this time forward, though the influence of Babylonian culture continued, Babylonian rule in the West was at an end. From the Tel el-Amarna correspondence we learn that the Babylonian Government was still inclined to intrigue in Palestine; the memories of its ancient empire were not altogether obliterated, and just as the English sovereigns called themselves kings of France long after they had ceased to possess an inch of French ground, so the Babylonian kings doubtless persuaded themselves that they were still by right the rulers of Canaan.

The wild mountaineers from the Kossæan highlands who had conquered Babylon soon passed under the spell of Babylonian culture, and became themselves Babylonian in habits, if not in name. They founded a dynasty which lasted for five hundred and seventy-six years and nine months. It is a curious

[1] This was "the year when Samsu-iluna the king gave Merodach a shining mace of gold and silver, the glory of the temple; it made E-Saggil (the temple of Bel-Merodach at Babylon) shine like the stars of heaven." The title of the year was derived from the chief event, or events, that characterized it. See Dr. Pinches, in the *Quarterly Statement of the Palestine Exploration Fund*, April and July 1900, pp. 269-73.

coincidence that Egypt also was governed about the same time by foreign conquerors, whose primitive wildness had been tamed by the influences of Egyptian civilization, which they had adopted as the Kossæan mountaineers adopted that of Babylonia, and whose rule also lasted for more than five hundred years. The Hyksos who conquered Egypt have been convincingly shown by recent discoveries to have been Semites, speaking a language of the West Semitic type.[1] They came from Canaan, and their conquest of Egypt made of it a dependency of Canaan. Hence they fixed their head-quarters in the northern part of their Egyptian territories, where they could easily keep up communication with Asia.

The excavations undertaken by the Palestine Exploration Fund at Lachish, Gezer and other sites in Southern Canaan have made it clear that throughout the Hyksos period Egypt and that part of Palestine were closely connected with one another. How much further eastward the government or influence of the Hyksos may have extended we do not know; the figure of a lion inscribed with the name of a Hyksos Pharaoh has been discovered in Babylonia, but this may have been brought from elsewhere. At any rate, so far as Palestine is concerned, we may say

[1] See my analysis of some of the Hyksos names in the *Proceedings of the Society of Biblical Archæology*, 1901, pp. 95–8. Since the publication of the Paper other names of the same type, like Rabu and Sakti, have come to light. The characteristic names of the Hyksos princes recur among the "Amorite" names found in the contract tablets of the Khammu-rabi period, but not later. The abbreviated forms of the names met with on the Egyptian scarabs are also found in the tablets. Indeed, the contracted form of Ya'qub-el, that is to say, Yakubu, with *k* instead of *q*, must have been transcribed from a cuneiform original.

that the Hyksos period in Egypt coincides with the disappearance of Babylonian rule in Canaan. From that time onward Canaan looks towards Egypt, and not towards Babylonia.

But even before the beginning of the Hyksos period Canaan—or at all events Southern Canaan—is Egyptian rather than Babylonian. That has been abundantly proved by Mr. Macalister's excavations at Gezer. Objects of the age of the Twelfth dynasty have been disinterred there, and of such a character as to make it evident that the country was already subject to Egyptian influence long before the appearance of the Hyksos. An Egyptian of that age was buried within the precincts of the consecrated " high place," and a stela commemorating him erected on the spot.

Both at Gezer and at Lachish it has been possible to trace the archæological chronology of the sites by the successive cities which arose upon them. Gezer was the older settlement of the two; its history goes back to the neolithic age, when it was inhabited by a race of short stature who lived in caves and burned their dead, and whose pottery was of the roughest description. Some of it was ornamented with streaks of red or black on a yellow or red wash, like coarse pottery of the age of the Third Egyptian dynasty which I have found in so-called " prehistoric " graves at El-Kab. Two settlements of the neolithic population can be made out, one resting upon the other ; in the second there was a distinct advance in civilization, and the place became a town surrounded by a wall. The neolithic race was succeeded by a taller race with Semitic characteristics, to whom the name of Amorite has been given; they buried the dead in a contracted position, and were acquainted with the use of copper and later of bronze. The city was now defended by a solid wall of stone, intersected with brick towers; as Mr. Macalister observes, in a country where stone is the natural building material the employment of brick must be due to foreign influence. He thinks the influence was Egyptian; this is very possible; but considering that building with brick was a salient feature in Babylonian civilization, the influence may have come rather from the side of Babylonia.

The first "Amorite" city at Gezer was coeval with the earliest city at Lachish—the modern Tel el-Hesy, where the Amorite settlers had no neolithic predecessors. At Gezer their sanctuary has been discovered. It was a "high place" formed of nine great monoliths running from north to south, and surrounded by a platform of large stones. The second monolith, polished with the kisses of the worshippers, was possibly the central object of veneration, the *bætylos* or *beth-el*, as it was termed.[1] This *beth-el*, or "house of God," takes us back to Semitic Babylonia. The veneration of isolated stones was common to all branches of the Semitic race; it may have come down to them from the days when their ancestors wandered over the desert plains of Arabia, where the solitary rocks assumed fantastic shapes that appealed to their imagination and excited

---

[1] Macalister, *Quarterly Statement of the Palestine Exploration Fund*, January 1903, p. 28. It is the seventh stone, however, which alone has been brought from a distance—the neighbourhood of Jerusalem—all the others being of local origin (*Quarterly Statement*, July 1904, pp. 194-5).

feelings of awe, while their shadows offered a welcome retreat in the heat of noon-day. In the historical age, however, it was not the rock itself that was adored, but the divinity whose home it had become by consecration with oil. The brick-built temple was called by the Babylonians a *bit-ili*, *beth-el*, or "house of God," and the name was easily transferred to the consecrated stones, the worship of which was coeval with the beginnings of Semitic history. But though the worship of stones was primitive, the belief that the stone was not a fetish, but the shrine of divinity, belonged to an age of reflection and points to a Babylonian source.

The first Amorite city at Gezer was succeeded by a second, in which the high place underwent enlargement and was provided with a temenos. Under its pavement have been found memorials of the grim rites performed in honour of its Baal—the bones of children and even adults who had been sacrificed and sometimes burnt and then deposited in jars. Similar sacrifices, it would seem, were offered when a new building was erected, since children's bones have been disinterred from under the foundations of houses, both at Gezer and at Taanach and Megiddo. The bones were placed in jars along with lamps and bowls, which, it has been suggested, were intended to receive the blood of the victim. The old sacred cave of the neolithic race was now brought into connection with the high place of the "Amorite" settlers, and the skeleton of a child has been found in it resting on a flat stone.

This fourth city at Gezer—the second since the Semites first settled there—has yielded objects which enable us to assign to it an approximate date. These objects are Egyptian, and belong to the age of the Twelfth dynasty. Many of them are scarabs, but there is also the tombstone of the Egyptian who was buried under the shadow of the Amorite sanctuary. Fragments of diorite and alabaster vases also occur, telling of trade with Egypt, and in the upper and later part of the stratum painted pottery makes its appearance similar to that met with in the corresponding stratum at Lachish. I shall have more to say about this painted pottery in the next chapter; here it is sufficient to state that it is related to the early painted pottery of the Ægean, but is itself of Hittite origin, and can be traced back to the Hittite centre in Cappadocia.

The fourth city had a long existence. It lasted from the period of the Twelfth Egyptian dynasty to the middle of the Eighteenth. Then it was ruined by an enemy and its old wall partially destroyed—doubtless by Thothmes III. when he conquered Palestine (about B.C. 1480). Upon its ruins rose another Amorite town. A new city wall was built of larger circumference and greater strength; it measured fourteen feet in thickness, and the stones of which it was composed were large and well shaped. The houses erected on the *débris* of the brick towers belonging to the old wall were filled with scarabs, beads, fragments of pottery and other objects contemporary with the reign of Amon-hotep III. (B.C. 1400). At Lachish the ruins of the third city were full of similar objects, and among them was a cuneiform tablet in which reference is made to the governor of Lachish mentioned in the Tel el-Amarna correspondence. At Taanach the

Austrian excavators discovered an archive-chamber, the contents of which were of the same age. Taanach was merely a third-rate or fourth-rate town, but its shêkh possessed a fortified residence, in a subterranean chamber of which his official records and private correspondence were kept in a coffer of terra-cotta. They were all in the Babylonian language and script. Among them is a list of the number of men each landowner (?) was required to furnish for the local militia, and there are also the letters which passed between the shêkh and his friends about their private affairs. How little of an official character is to be found in these letters may be gathered from the following translation of one of them : "To Istar-yisur (writes) Guli-Hadad.—Live happily! May the gods grant health to yourself, your house and your sons! You have written to me about the money . . . and behold I will give fifty pieces of silver, since this has not (yet) been done.—Again : Why have you sent your salutation here afresh? All you have heard there I have (already) learned through Bel-ram.— Again : If the finger of the goddess Asherat appears, let them announce (the omen) and observe (it), and you shall describe to me both the sign and the fact. As to your daughter, we know the one, Salmisa, who is in the city of Rabbah, and if she grows up, you must give her to the prince ; she is in truth fit for a lord."[1]

These Taanach letters are a final proof, if any were needed, of the completely Babylonian nature of Canaanitish civilization in the century before the

[1] See Sellin, *Tell Ta'annek* (1904) and *Eine Nachlese auf dem Tell Ta'annek in Palästina* (1905).

BABYLONIA AND PALESTINE 151

Exodus. When we find the petty shêkhs of obscure Canaanite towns corresponding with one another on the trivial matters of every-day life in the foreign language and syllabary of Babylonia, it is evident that Babylonian influence was still as strong in Palestine as it had been in the days when "the land of the Amorites" was a Babylonian province. It is also evident that there must have been plenty of schools in which the foreign language and syllabary could be taught and studied, and that the clay literature of Babylonia had been carried to the West. Indeed the Tel el-Amarna collection contains proof of this latter fact. Along with the letters are fragments of Babylonian literary works, one of which has been interpunctuated in order to facilitate its reading by the Egyptian scholar.

On the other hand, apart from the cuneiform tablets the more strictly archæological evidence of Babylonian influence upon Canaan is extraordinarily scanty. Naturally we should discover no traces of "the goodly Babylonish garments" which, as we learn from the Book of Joshua, were imported into the country, the climate of Palestine not being favourable to their preservation; but it is certainly strange that so few seal-cylinders or similar objects have been disinterred, either at Gezer and Lachish in the south, or at Taanach and Megiddo in the north. What makes it the stranger is that Mr. Macalister has opened a long series of graves, beginning with the neolithic race and coming down to Græco-Roman times, and that while the influence of Egypt is sufficiently visible in them, that of Babylonia is almost entirely absent. It is true that a few seal-cylinders have been met with in the excavations on the city sites, but with the exception of one found at Taanach[1] I do not know of any that can be said to be of purely Babylonian manufacture; most of them are of Syrian make, and represent a Syrian modification of the Babylonian type. And yet there are seal-cylinders from the Lebanon, now in the Ashmolean Museum at Oxford, which are purely Babylonian in origin, and belong to the period of Khammu-rabi.[2] There are also two seal-cylinders of later pattern in M. de Clercq's collection, on which are representations of the Egyptian gods Set and Horus—similar to those found on scarabs from the Delta of the time of the Eighteenth and Nineteenth dynasties—as well as of the Canaanite god Reshef, accompanied by cuneiform inscriptions which on palæographic grounds must be assigned to the age of the Tel el-Amarna tablets. As the inscriptions record the names of Hadad-sum and his son Anniy, "citizens of Sidon, the crown of the gods," we know that they have come from the Phœnician coast.[3] Like the cuneiform tablets, they bear witness to the long-continued influence of Babylonian culture in Canaan on its literary side.

When we turn to theology and law, the same influence is recognizable. The deities of Canaan were to a large extent Babylonian, with Babylonian names. The Babylonian gods Ana, Nebo, Rimmon (Rammân), Hadad and Dagon meet us in the names

---

[1] *Tell Ta'annek*, pp. 27-8. The cylinder is earlier than B.C. 2000.

[2] See my *Patriarchal Palestine*, pp. 60, 61.

[3] *Collection De Clercq, Catalogue méthodique et raisonné*, i. p. 217.

of places and persons, and Ashtoreth, who shared with Baal the devotion of the inhabitants of Palestine, is the Babylonian Istar with the suffix of the feminine attached to her name. Even Asherah, in whom Semitic scholars were long inclined to see a genuinely Canaanitish goddess, turns out to have been of Babylonian origin, and to be the feminine counterpart of Asir, or Asur, the national god of Assyria. The recently-discovered legal code of Khammu-rabi has shown that such glimpses as we have in the Book of Genesis of the laws and legal customs of Canaan in the patriarchal age all presuppose Babylonian law. From time to time usages are referred to and laws implied which have no parallel in the Mosaic code, and are therefore presumably pre-Israelite. But though they have no parallel in the Mosaic code, we have now learnt that they were all provided for in the code of Khammu-rabi. Thus Abram's adoption of his slave and house-steward Eliezer is in strict accordance with the provisions of the old Babylonian law. Adoption, indeed, which was practically unknown among the Israelites, was a leading feature in Babylonian life, and the childless man was empowered to adopt an heir, even from among his slaves, to whom he left his name and his property. So, again, Sarai's conduct in regard to Hagar, or Rachel's conduct in regard to Bilhah, is explained by the Babylonian enactment which allowed the wife to present her husband with a concubine ; while we can now understand why Hagar was not sold after her quarrel with Sarai, for the Babylonian law laid down that "if a man has married a wife, and she has given a concubine to her husband by whom he

has had a child, should the concubine afterwards
have a dispute with her mistress because she has
borne children, her mistress cannot sell her; she can
only lay a task upon her and make her live with the
other slaves."

In the account of Isaac's marriage with Rebekah
it is again a provision of the old Babylonian code
with which we meet. There we hear of the bride
receiving a dowry from the father of the bridegroom,
and of other presents being made to her mother in con-
formity with Babylonian usage. So, too, the infliction
of death by burning with which Judah threatened
his daughter-in-law Tamar, on the supposition that
she was a widow, has its explanation in the legislation
of Khammu-rabi, where the same punishment is
enacted against a nun who has been unfaithful to
her vows of virginity or widowhood. The story of
the purchase of the cave of Machpelah, moreover,
has long been recognized by Assyriologists as pre-
supposing an acquaintance with the legal forms of
a Babylonian sale of land in the Khammu-rabi age.

With all this heritage of Babylonian culture, therefore, it is curious that the excavators in Palestine
have come across so few material evidences of intercourse with Babylonia. Mr. Macalister is inclined to
believe that it must belong to a period anterior to
the Twelfth Egyptian dynasty. But this raises a
chronological question of some difficulty. We have
seen that the earlier and inner city wall of Gezer
served as the defence of three successive settlements,
and that it was partially destroyed along with the
city it protected about B.C. 1480. Now the outer and
more massive wall which superseded it also served

to protect three cities, the latest of which was deserted during the Maccabean period, about B.C. 100. Hence, Mr. Macalister argues, "if we may assume the rate of growth to have been fairly uniform, we are led back to B.C. 2900 as the (latest) date" for the foundation of the first wall. During this long period of time twenty-eight feet of *débris* accumulated ; below this are as much as twelve feet of neolithic accumulation.[1]

The conquests of Sargon of Akkad would accordingly have fallen within the neolithic epoch. But in this case it is strange that the use of copper, with which Babylonia had long been acquainted, was not communicated to its Western province, and that it should have needed a new race and the lapse of nearly a thousand years for its introduction. Moreover, specific evidences of Babylonian civilization are quite as much wanting in the remains of the first Amorite city as they are in those of the second. And unless we adopt a date for the Twelfth Egyptian dynasty, which on other grounds seems out of the question, it is hard to see how the Khammu-rabi dynasty can be placed before it. What little evidence we possess at present goes to indicate that the Khammu-rabi dynasty was contemporaneous with the earlier Hyksos kings or their immediate predecessors. And yet not only do we know that the Khammu-rabi dynasty ruled in Palestine, but the adoption of the cuneiform script, which was at least as old as the age of that dynasty, as well as the testimony of theology and law, proves that its rule

[1] *Quarterly Statement of the Palestine Exploration Fund*, January 1905, pp. 28, 29.

156 ARCHÆOLOGY OF CUNEIFORM INSCRIPTIONS

must have exercised a profound and permanent influence upon the people of Canaan. How is it, then, that while the excavations have brought to light so many evidences of Egyptian domination, there is so little in the way of material objects to show that Palestine was once and for several centuries a Babylonian province?[1]

Perhaps the excavations which are still proceeding at Megiddo may throw some light upon the problem. Meanwhile, we may remember that thus far the greater part of the objects that have been found belong to the less wealthy and educated part of the population. The annals of Thothmes III. prove that, so far as the upper classes were concerned, the picture of Canaanitish luxury presented in the Old Testament had a foundation of fact. Among the spoils taken from the princes of Canaan we hear of tables, chairs and staves of cedar and ebony inlaid or gilded with gold, of a golden plough and sceptre, of richly-embroidered stuffs similar to those depicted on the walls of the Egyptian monuments, of chariots chased with silver, of iron tent-poles studded with precious stones, and of "bowls with goats' heads on them, and one with a lion's head, the workmanship of the land

---

[1] The chronological difficulty, however, would be partially solved if the date recently proposed by Professor Petrie (*Researches in Sinai*, ch. xii.) for the Twelfth dynasty—B.C. 3459-3250—be adopted. The Twelfth dynasty would in this case have reigned a thousand years before the dynasty of Khammu-rabi, whose domination in Palestine would have been an interlude in the history of the Hyksos period, while the conquest of Canaan by Sargon and Naram-Sin would have coincided with the supersession of the neolithic population by the "Amorites," who brought with them the copper and the culture of Babylonia.

of the Zahi," that is to say, of the Canaanitish coast. These latter were doubtless imitations of the gold and silver cups with double handles and animals' heads imported from Krete, which were also received as tribute from the Canaanitish princes by the Egyptian king. Other gifts comprised chariots plated with gold, iron armour with gold inlay, a helmet of gold inlaid with lapis-lazuli, the tusks of elephants, rings of gold and silver that were used as money, copper and lead, as well as jars of wine, oil and balsam. Of all these articles, the copper and lead excepted, it is needless to say next to nothing has been discovered by the excavators. The most valuable work of art yet met with is a bronze sword of precisely the same shape as one found in Assyria, which bears upon it the name of Hadad-nirari I. (B.C. 1330).[1]

On the palæographical side the forms of the cuneiform characters used in Canaan go back to the script of the age of Khammu-rabi and his predecessors. From a purely Assyriological point of view, no regard being had to other considerations, I should date their introduction into Palestine about B.C. 2300. The chronology that would best harmonize the historical facts would thus be one which made the dominance of Egypt in Palestine under the Twelfth dynasty precede the Babylonian rule of the Khammu-rabi period. Against it is the negative

[1] Unless we except the gold and silver ornaments found on the body of a woman in a deserted house at Taanach, which, as Dr. Sellin says, are by themselves sufficient to remove "all grounds for doubting such accounts as those in Joshua vii. 21, and Judges viii. 26" (*Eine Nachlese auf dem Tell Ta'annek*, p. 32).

evidence of archæological discovery, so few traces of this rule having been discovered in the course of the excavations. But neither in archæology nor in anything else is negative evidence of much value.

At any rate, thanks to the decipherment of the cuneiform inscriptions, the main facts are clear. Canaan was once a province of the Babylonian Empire, and during the long period of time that this was the case it became permeated with the literary culture of Babylonia. The civilization which was partially destroyed by the Israelitish invasion had its roots in the valley of the Euphrates.

Gezer, it is true, was one of the cities in which no visible break with the past was made by the irruption of the desert tribes. It escaped capture by the invaders, and it was only in the reign of Solomon, when the Israelites had already entered into the heritage of the old Canaanitish culture, that it was handed over by the king of Egypt to his Jewish son-in-law. But at Lachish the marks of the destruction of the town by Joshua are still visible. Above the ruins of the Amorite cities is a bed of ashes left by the charcoal-burners who squatted on the site before it was again rebuilt. Above the stratum of ashes all must be Israelitish, and the objects found in the remains of the cities that stand upon it testify accordingly to a complete change. No more cuneiform tablets are met with, and but few Egyptian scarabs; the pottery is different, and the "high place" has disappeared. The bowl and lamp, indeed, are still buried under the walls of the newly-built house, but the bones of sacrificed children which they once contained are replaced by sand. As the Israelitish power increased the old Babylonian influence necessarily lessened. When the cuneiform syllabary finally made way for the so-called Phœnician alphabet is still uncertain, but it was at all events before the days of Solomon. Already in the Amorite period the characters of the Kretan linear script discovered by Dr. Evans are found scratched on fragments of pottery, indicating that besides the cuneiform another form of writing was known ; it may be that the Israelitish conquest, by destroying the centres of Canaanitish civilization and the schools of the scribes, gave a first blow to the tradition of Babylonian learning, and that the work of destruction was subsequently completed by the Philistine wars.

CHAPTER VI

ASIA MINOR

IF it has been a surprise to learn that Palestine was once within the circle of Babylonian culture, it has been equally a surprise to learn that Asia Minor was so too. It is true that Herodotus traced the Herakleid dynasty of Lydian kings to the gods of Nineveh and Babylon, that Strabo knew of a " mound of Semiramis " in Cappadocia, and that in the Book of Genesis Lud is called the son of Shem. But historians had long agreed that all such beliefs were creations of a later day, and rested on no substratum of fact. The northern limits of Babylonian or Assyrian influence, it was held, were fixed by the Taurus and the mountains of Kurdistan.

The discovery of cuneiform inscriptions on the stones and rocks of Armenia made the first breach in this conclusion. Their existence was known even before Botta and Layard had opened up Nineveh. In 1826 Schulz had been sent by the French Government at the instance of M. Mohl to copy the mysterious characters which had already excited the attention of Oriental writers. Schulz was unexpectedly successful in his quest. The number of inscriptions he discovered was far larger than had been imagined, and his copies of them, as we now know, were remarkably accurate. But the explorer himself never lived to return to Europe. He was murdered by a Kurdish chief, Nurallah Bey, in 1829, while engaged in the work of exploration; his papers, however, were eventually recovered, and the inscriptions he had copied were published in 1840 in the Journal of the Société Asiatique. One of them was a trilingual inscription of Xerxes, the Persian transcript of which was just beginning to be deciphered ; the rest were still a closed book.

Then came the discovery of Nineveh and the first essays at the interpretation of the Assyro-Babylonian texts. Layard himself made an expedition to Armenia, and besides recopying Schulz's texts and correcting certain inaccuracies in them, added considerably to the collection. Dr. Hincks, with his usual genius for decipherment, perceived that the syllabary in which they were written was the same as that used at Nineveh, and utilized them for determining the values of some of the Assyrian characters. He succeeded in reading most of the proper names, in assigning the inscriptions to a group of kings whose order he was able to fix, and in pointing out that many of them contain an account of military campaigns and of the amount of booty which had been carried off. But it was also clear that the inscriptions were not in a Semitic language, and as the nominative and accusative of the noun seemed to terminate in -s and -n, while the patronymic was expressed by the suffix -khinis, the decipherer assumed that the language was Indo-European. The most important texts had been found in or near Van, which

L

had apparently been the capital of the kings by whose orders they had been engraved, and the name of Vannic, accordingly, was given to both texts and language.

It was soon recognized that Dr. Hincks had been in error in suggesting that the Vannic language was Indo-European. It was, it is true, inflectional, but with this any resemblance to the languages of the Indo-European family ceased. Nor was there any other language or group of languages to which it appeared to be related, and all attempts failed to advance the decipherment much beyond the point at which it had been left by Hincks. Thanks to the "determinatives," which indicate proper names and the like, and the ideographs, which are fairly plentiful, the general sense of many of the inscriptions could be made out; but beyond that it seemed impossible to go. Lenormant, indeed, following Hincks, showed that the suffix *-bi* denoted the first person singular of the verb, and indicated Georgian as possibly a related language; but in the hands of other would-be decipherers, like Robert and Mordtmann, there was retrogression instead of advance.

So matters remained until 1882, when Stanislas Guyard pointed out the parallelism between a formula which occurs at the end of many Vannic inscriptions and the imprecatory formula of the Assyrian texts. I had already been struck by the same fact, and was at the time preparing a Memoir on the decipherment and translation of the inscriptions, which shortly afterwards appeared in the *Journal of the Royal Asiatic Society*. In this I had made use of Layard's copies, which had never been published; other copies also, including photographs, squeezes and casts, had been placed at my disposal, and in 1882 I was able to lay before cuneiform scholars a grammar and vocabulary of the Vannic language, together with translations and analyses of all the known texts.[1] These have been subsequently corrected and extended by other Assyriologists—Guyard, D. H. Müller, Nikolsky, Scheil, Belck and Lehmann, as well as by myself. An ordinary Vannic text can now be translated with nearly as much completeness and certainty as an Assyrian text, and the number of them known to us has been greatly enlarged by the archæological explorations of Belck and Lehmann.

In the decipherment of the Vannic inscriptions the ideographs and determinatives which are scattered through them ook the place for me of a bilingual text. The determinatives told me what was the nature of the words which followed or preceded them, and so explained the general sense of the passages in which they occurred, while from time to time a phonetically-written word would be replaced in a parallel passage by an ideograph the signification of which was known. I soon found, moreover, that the cuneiform syllabary must have been brought from Nineveh to Van in the age of Assur-natsir-pal II. (B.C. 884–859), and that the actual phrases met with in the inscriptions of that monarch are sometimes reproduced in a Vannic dress. The Vannic language, however, still remains isolated, though the majority of those who have studied it incline to Lenormant's view that its nearest living representative is Georgian. Not being a Georgian

[1] *Journal of the Royal Asiatic Society*, New Series, xiv. 3, 4, pp. 377–732.

scholar myself, this is a point upon which I can express no opinion.

Instead of " Vannic," it has been proposed to call the language " Khaldian." The chief god of the people who spoke the language was Khaldis, and in the inscriptions we find the people themselves described as " the children of Khaldis." Derivatives from the name are found employed in a geographical sense northward of the region to which the inscriptions belong. Thus the Khaldi " in the neighbourhood of Colchis " are said to have been also called Khaldæi ;[1] " Khaldees " are frequently referred to by Armenian writers as living between Trapezont and Batûm, and a Turkish inscription at Sumela shows that as late as the beginning of the fifteenth century Lazistân was still known as Khaldia. That the name was ever applied, however, to the kingdom which had its chief seat at Van is not proved, and it is therefore best to adhere to the term " Vannic," which commits those who use it to no theory.[2]

The decipherment of the Vannic texts has not only led to the discovery of a new language, it has also thrown a flood of light on the early history, geography and religion of the Armenian plateau. The military campaigns of the Assyrian kings had brought it into contact with Assyrian civilization, and in the ninth century before our era a dynasty arose which adopted the literary culture and art of Assyria, and founded a powerful kingdom which extended its sway from Urumia on the east to Malatia on the west, and from

[1] Eustathius on Dion. Perieget. 767. See Lehmann in the *Zeitschrift für Assyriologie*, 1894, pp. 90 and 358–60.

[2] The Vannic kings always call themselves kings, not of the Khaldians, but of Biainas or Bianas, the Byana of Ptolemy, the Van of to-day.

the slopes of Ararat and the shores of Lake Erivan to
the northern frontiers of Assyria.

The main fact which has thus been disclosed is that
the Armenians of history—the Aryan tribes, that is
to say, who spoke an Indo-European language—did
not enter the country and establish themselves in the
place of its older rulers before the end of the seventh
century before our era. The fall of the Vannic monarchy seems to have coincided with the fall of the
Assyrian Empire, with which it had once contended
on almost equal terms, and in each case the invasion
of the so-called Scythian hordes from the plains of
Eastern Europe had much to do with the result. The
founders of Armenian civilization and of the cities of
the Armenian plateau had no connection with the
Indo-European family. Their type of language corresponded with that which distinguishes most of the
actual languages of the Caucasus, though no genetic
relationship is traceable between them. The break
with the past, however, occasioned by the irruption of
the Indo-European invaders, was so great that not
only did the older language become extinct and forgotten, but even the tradition of the older civilization
was also lost. Like the recovery of the Sumerian
language and the culture it represented, the recovery
of the Vannic language and culture is the revelation
of a new world.

At the head of the pantheon was a trinity consisting of Khaldis, the supreme god of the race; Teisbas,
the god of the air; and the Sun-god Ardinis. Temples
were erected in their honour, and shields and spears
dedicated to their service. The vine, which grows
wild in Armenia, was the sacred tree of the people,

and there are inscriptions which commemorate its planting and consecration, and describe the endowments that were set apart for its maintenance. Wine was naturally offered to the gods along with the domestic animals and prisoners of war. Dr. Belck has discovered burial-places which go back to the neolithic age, but the majority of the monuments scattered over the Vannic area belong to the bronze age, and testify to a native adaptation of Assyrian art and culture. Iron also makes its appearance, but scantily. The pottery of the age of the inscriptions is related on the one side to the Assyrian pottery of the same period, and on the other to the pottery of Asia Minor. The polished red ware more especially points to the west.[1]

The existence of a language of the Caucasian type in Armenia, and its association with a powerful kingdom and an advanced culture, is not the only revelation of the kind that we owe to cuneiform decipherment. We have learned that at a much earlier epoch Northern Mesopotamia was occupied by a people who spoke a language of similar type but of far more complicated form; and that here, too, the language in question was accompanied by a high civilization, a

---

[1] See more especially Belck's comparison of the Vannic pottery with that of the Assyrian colony of Kara Eyuk, near Kaisariyeh, in the *Verhandlungen der Berliner anthropologischen Gesellschaft*, December 1901, p. 493. Besides the highly-polished lustrous red ware, he found at Kara Eyuk fragments of the same wheel-made wine-jars, "of gigantic size," which characterized Toprak Kaleh, near Van. Similar jars, as well as lustrous red pottery, were discovered by Schliemann in the "prehistoric" strata at Troy. The animals' heads in terra-cotta found at Kara Eyuk are stated by Dr. Belck to be similar to those of the Digalla Tepé, near Urumiya. For further details see *infra*.

powerful monarchy, and the use of the cuneiform syllabary. The monarchy was that of Mitanni, and its culture and script had been borrowed from Babylonia in the age of Khammu-rabi, instead of from Assyria in the age of Assur-natsir-pal. But it is interesting to observe that in borrowing the script the people of Mitanni had adapted and simplified it in precisely the same way as did the people of Van in after days. Superfluous characters were discarded, a single phonetic value only assigned to each character, and large use made of those which expressed vowels. In fact, in both Mitannian and Vannic the system of writing begins to approach the alphabetic. Whether this similarity in adaptation was due to a similarity of phonetic structure in the two languages or to conscious imitation on the part of the Vannic scribes it is difficult to say ; it is a point, however, which cannot be passed over.

The name of Mitanni meets us on the Egyptian monuments of the Eighteenth and Nineteenth dynasties. The kingdom played a considerable part at that period of time in the politics of Western Asia, and the daughters of its kings were married to the Egyptian Pharaohs. The boundaries of the Egyptian Empire were coterminous with those of Mitanni, and we gather from the Tel el-Amarna correspondence that the Mitannian forces had more than once made their way into Palestine, perhaps as far south as Jerusalem, and that Mitannian intrigue was active in that portion of the Pharaoh's dominions. Among the Canaanitish governors are some who bear Mitannian names, and testify to the continuance of a Mitannian element in that common meeting-place of nationalities.

Several letters from the Mitannian king have been found among the Tel el-Amarna tablets. Most oĺ them are written in the Babylonian language, but one —and fortunately an exceptionally long one—though in cuneiform characters, is in the native language of the country. A comparison of it with its companion letters, assisted by the determinatives and ideographs which are employed in it from time to time, has enabled Jensen, Leopold Messerschmidt and myself to decipher a very considerable part of the letter, and so to compile a grammar and vocabulary of the Mitannian language. That it is distantly related to Vannic seems to admit of little doubt, but it comes before us in a much more developed form ; indeed, its system of suffixes is so elaborate and ponderous as to remind us of the polysynthetic languages of America.

A legal document found in Babylonia and dated in the epoch of Khammu-rabi contains a number of proper names which are of Mitannian or allied origin, and show that persons of that race were already settled in Babylonia.[1] As the Mitannian form of cuneiform script must have been borrowed about the same time, we may infer that the advanced guard of the northern race had already made its way as far south as Mesopotamia, and there established its power in the midst of a Semitic population. From that time forward a constant struggle went on between the two races, the Semitic race striving to push back the northern intruders and planting its own colonies in the very heart of the northern area,

---

[1] See Pinches in the *Journal of the Royal Asiatic Society*, 1897, pp. 589–613 ; and myself in the *Proceedings of the Society of Biblical Archæology*, 1897, p. 286.

while the northerners pressed ever more and more to the southward, and at one time even seemed likely to possess themselves of the heritage of the Babylonian Empire in Western Asia. Like Armenia, Northern Mesopotamia was occupied by a people of Caucasian and Asianic affinities, whose armies had crossed the Euphrates and won territory in Syria and Palestine.

On the west, however, the Mitannians found themselves confronted by another northern population, the Hittites, whose first home was in Cappadocia. The Hittites also had passed under the spell of Babylonian culture, and the cuneiform script had been carried to them at an early date. Thanks to recent discoveries, we can now trace in some measure the earlier fortunes of a race who made a profound impression, not only on the future history of Asia Minor and its relations with Greece, but also on the history of Palestine.

As far back as about B.C. 2000, Babylonian or Assyrian troops had already made their way along the northern banks of the Tigris and Euphrates to the borders of Cappadocia and the neighbourhood of the Halys. I say Babylonian or Assyrian, for Assyria was at the time a province of Babylonia, though as the colonies which settled in the track of the invaders were distinctively Assyrian in their municipal customs and the names of their inhabitants, the troops were probably drafted from Assyria.[1] The mineral wealth of Cappadocia was doubtless the attraction which led them to such distant and semi-

[1] Thus we find from the Cappadocian cuneiform tablets discovered at Kara Eyuk, north-east of Kaisariyeh, that time was reckoned by the annual succession of officers called *limmi* as in Assyria.

barbarous lands; Dr. Gladstone's analysis of the gold
of the Sixth Egyptian dynasty, with its admixture of
silver, has shown that it was imported from the north
of Asia Minor,[1] and the silver itself was probably
already worked. Further south, in the Taurus, were
mines of copper.

However this may be, the remains of one of these
early Assyro-Babylonian colonies has been partially
excavated a few miles (twenty-three kilometres) to the
north-east of Kaisariyeh.[2] The site is now known as
Kara Eyuk, "the Black Mound," and numerous cuneiform tablets have come from it. It has obtained its
present name from the marks of fire which are everywhere visible upon it, and bear eloquent testimony to its
final fate. Established as an outpost of the Assyrian
Empire in the distant west, a time came when, deserted by the Government at home, its strong walls
were battered down by the besieging foe and the
Assyrian settlers massacred among the ruins of their
burning town. According to M. Chantre, its excavator (who, however, believes that it was destroyed
by a volcanic eruption), the whole mound is a mass of
charred and burnt remains.

The construction of the walls, as well as the pottery
found within them, marks it off with great distinctness
from the ruins of the Hittite or native Cappadocian
cities in its neighbourhood. While in their case the
city wall is made of unmortared blocks of stone, the
walls of Kara Eyuk are built of brick, and where
stones are used they are of small size and cemented
with mortar. The pottery differs considerably from

---

[1] *Dendereh*, p. 62.
[2] Chantre, *Mission en Cappadoce*, pp. 71-91.

that of the Hittite capital at Boghaz Keui. Some of it is of black ware, especially characterized by the vases with long spouts, which are also found in Phrygia and the Troad. Some of it, again, is of the dark-red lustrous ware which has been met with at Toprak Kaleh, near Van, and Boz Eyuk in Phrygia, while the yellow ware with geometrical patterns in black and maroon-red which has been discovered in Phrygia occurs in large quantities. This latter ware is of the class known as " Mykenæan."[1]

The cuneiform tablets which have come from the site are known as " Cappadocian," and were first noticed by Dr. Pinches. The forms of the characters resemble those of the early Babylonian script, which was still used in Assyria in the age of Khammu-rabi. Many of the proper names, moreover, seem to be dis-

[1] See Belck, *Verhandlungen der Berliner anthropologischen Gesellschaft*, December 1901, p. 493 ; and the admirable plates, iii., vii.–xiv., in Chantre, *Mission en Cappadoce*. As has been already mentioned (*supra*, p. 166), Dr. Belck noticed at Kara Eyuk coarse sherds of great thickness coming from wine-jars similar to those of Toprak Kaleh. The black vases with long spouts have been found at Yortan and Boz Eyuk in Phrygia ; long-spouted vases of yellow ware with geometrical patterns in maroon-red on the site of Gordium.

Chantre discovered numerous spindle-whorls in the ruins similar to those discovered at Troy. He also found terra-cotta figurines, among which the ram is the most plentiful, as well as covers and handles of vases in the shape of animals' heads, and some curious hut-urns not unlike those of Latium. Few bronze objects were met with, but among them were five flanged axe-heads of the incurved Egyptian Hyksos type, totally unlike the straight bronze axe-heads from Troy and Angora (of Egyptian I–XII dynasty form), with which M. Chantre compares them. The obsidian implements and stone celts were of the ordinary Asianic pattern. M. Chantre notes that whereas at Troy the terra-cotta figurines represented the heads of oxen or cows, at Kara Eyuk they were the heads of sheep, horses, and perhaps dogs.

tinctive of that period. On the other hand, a large proportion of them contain the name of Asur—often in its primitive form of Asir—or are otherwise characteristic of Assyria. The tablets are further dated by the archons who gave their names to the years, a system of chronology which was peculiar to Assyria and unknown in Babylonia, while the month was divided into "weeks" of five days each. The language of the tablets also, which is full of dialectic mispronunciations and strange words, points to Assyria rather than to the southern kingdom, and we may therefore conclude that the colonists were Assyrians, even though the colony may have been founded when Assyria was still a Babylonian province.

There are indications in the Assyrian inscriptions themselves that the road to Cappadocia was known to the Assyrian princes at an early epoch. The earliest Assyrian kings whose annals have come down to us are Hadad-nirari I. and his son Shalmaneser I. (B.C. 1300). Hadad-nirari tells us that his great-grandfather, Assur-yuballidh, whose letters form part of the Tel el-Amarna correspondence, had subdued "the wide-spread" province of Subari, which lay near the sources of the Euphrates, and in which Kara Eyuk was perhaps included, while he himself restored the cities of the same province which had fallen into ruin. Later, Shalmaneser I. conducted campaign after campaign towards the same region. In his second year he overthrew the king of Malatia, and the combined forces of the other "Hittite" states, who had come to his assistance : "all were conquered," from the borders of Cappadocia to the Hittite stronghold of Carchemish. A military colony was settled at the head waters of the Tigris which secured the high-road to Asia Minor.

Two centuries later we learn from Tiglath-pileser I. that Moschians and Hittites had overrun part of this Assyrian territory, and occupied some of the Assyrian settlements. Once more, therefore, the Assyrian troops marched to the north-west; the provinces which lay in the valley of the Murad-chai were recovered, and the old province of Subari cleared of intruders. Soon afterwards Tiglath-pileser forced his way into Southern Cappadocia and the valley of the Sarus, making Comana tributary, razing to the ground the fortresses that had resisted him, and erecting on their site chambers of brick, with bronze tablets on which his conquests were recorded. Eastern Cilicia was known at the time to the Assyrians as Muzri, or "the Marchland," a clear proof that it had long formed a borderland and debatable territory between the Assyrian Empire and the nations of Asia Minor.

It is thus evident that even before the rise of the Assyrian monarchy, the road that led to the mining districts of Cappadocia, along the valleys of the Upper Tigris, Euphrates and Tokhma Su, was not only known to the Assyro-Babylonians, but had actually constituted Assyrian territory, which was colonized by Assyrian garrisons and paid tribute to Nineveh whenever Assyria was strong enough to enforce its authority. At the eastern extremity of the road stood the city of unknown name, now represented by "the Burnt Mound" of Kara Eyuk, whose existence as an Assyro-Babylonian city probably dates back to the age of Khammu-rabi.

It was the outpost of Babylonian culture in Asia

Minor. Babylonian art, and, above all, the Babylonian system of writing, were brought by it into the heart of the Hittite region, and the archæological objects found there consequently become important for chronological dating. Not far off, on the other side of the Halys, rose the Hittite capital, now known as Boghaz Keui, the centre from which, as Professor Ramsay has shown,[1] the early roads of Asia Minor radiated in all directions.

Boghaz Keui still awaits the scientific excavator ; but fragments of cuneiform tablets have been picked up on its site by M. Chantre and Dr. Belck, and last year I obtained at Constantinople a large and important one which is now at Liverpool. The language of the tablets is not Assyrian, but that spoken by the native inhabitants of the country. As in Armenia, the cuneiform script was borrowed along with other elements of Babylonian culture ; but it was adapted to express the language of its borrowers.

By one of those coincidences which sometimes happen in archæological research, the discovery fits with another fact which had long been in the possession of the Assyriologist, though the full meaning of it was unknown to him. Among the Tel el-Amarna letters are two in a language unlike any with which we are acquainted. One of them is from a Hittite leader of condottieri,[2] who has left us two other letters which

---

[1] *Historical Geography of Asia Minor*, ch. i., ii. ; *Cities and Bishoprics of Phrygia*, i. p. xiv.

[2] Labawa, or Labbaya, for whom see the next chapter. A revised transcript of his letter in Arzawan (Hittite) is given by Knudtzon, *Die zwei Arzawa-Briefe*, pp. 38–40. The introductory paragraph should read : *Ata-mu kit Labbaya . . memis-ta Uan-wa-nnas iskhani-tta-ra atari-ya ueni.*—" To

are in the Assyrian language, and who came from a town in the neighbourhood of Cilicia. The second letter was written to the king of Arzawa by one of the foreign secretaries of the Egyptian Government. But the situation of Arzawa was wholly uncertain; as the king bore the Hittite name of Tarkhundaraba, I suggested that it lay in the Hittite territory, and that consequently in the language of the letter we had a fragment of the Hittite language. For many years, however, this remained a mere conjecture, without any definite proofs.

When the fragmentary tablets from Boghaz Keui came to be copied, it was at once perceived that they were in a language which resembled that of the Arzawa letters, but it was not until the new tablet from Constantinople had been cleaned and copied by Dr. Pinches and myself that the actual facts became clear. The Arzawa and Boghaz Keui texts agree in the forms given to the characters, in grammar and in vocabulary. Arzawa, therefore, must have been the Hittite kingdom which had its centre at Boghaz Keui, and already in the age of the Eighteenth Egyptian dynasty it was employing a form of the cuneiform script which implied a long preceding period of use and adaptation. A new realm has thus to be added to the domain of the cuneiform system of writing; in Syria the Hittite king of Kadesh wrote to the Pharaoh in Babylonian, but in his old home in the north, though the Babylonian

---

my lord says Labbaya . . . . thy servant of Uan (a district west of Aleppo) ; seven times I prostrate myself." In other letters Labbaya is called prince of Rukhizzi, the Rokhe's-na of the treaty between Ramses II. and the Hittites.

syllabary had been adopted, the language it served to express was that of the Hittites themselves.

A certain amount of this Hittite language of Arzawa can be deciphered, thanks to those same determinatives and ideographs which have assisted so materially towards the decipherment of the Vannic texts, and more especially to the recurrence in the two Tel el-Amarna letters of phrases that are common to the whole correspondence. The new tablet, however, is more than usually helpful, since it contains Assyrian words and grammatical forms which in parallel passages of the same text are replaced by native equivalents. In this way a sketch of Arzawan grammar can now be made, as well as a list of Arzawan words. The language which is thus disclosed is of an Asianic type, with features that remind us of Lycian on the one side, and of Mitannian and Vannic on the other. But in what may be termed the fundamentals of grammar it agrees with Mitannian and Vannic.

At the same time, certain of these same fundamentals have a curious but superficial resemblance to what we have hitherto been accustomed to regard as characteristics of Indo-European grammar. The nominative and accusative of the noun, for example, are distinguished by the suffixes -*s* and -*n*, the plural nominative and accusative often terminate in -*s*, and the possessive pronouns of Arzawan are *mi-s*, "mine"; *ti-s*, "thine"; and *sa(s)*, "his"; while *si* is "(to) her." The third person of the present tense ends in -*t*; *es-tu*, is "may it be"; *es-mi*, "may I be." Yet with all these remarkable coincidences, I can assure the comparative philologist that Arzawan is certainly not an Indo-

European language, and I must leave him to explain them as best he may.

We have, however, learnt a good deal more about the Hittite populations of Asia Minor from the Tel el-Amarna tablets than the nature of the language which they spoke. In the closing days of the Eighteenth Egyptian dynasty we find them on the southern side of the Taurus, sending forth bands of adventurers, who hired their services to the king of Egypt and to the rival governors and princes of Palestine, and from time to time carved out principalities of their own with the sword. We are even able to follow the fortunes of some of the leaders of the condottieri, who had no scruple in transferring their allegiance from one vassal prince to another when tempted by the prospect of better pay, or in murdering their employer when the opportunity arose, and plundering or occupying his city. They had, it is true, a wholesome awe of Egyptian power and of the Egyptian army, and some of the letters they wrote to the Egyptian court are amusing examples of the excuses they offered for their misdeeds. But they never hesitated about seizing the Pharaoh's property when they thought they could do so with impunity, while they were all the time professing to be his devoted slaves. A considerable number of the vassal princes of Canaan kept these mercenaries in their pay, and in many cases the Egyptian Foreign Office thought it wisest to confirm one of their leaders in the government of a district, however doubtful might have been the means by which it had come into his hands. So long as the tribute was paid, and the imperial authority acknowledged, no further questions

M

were asked. The mercenaries were useful at times to the imperial forces, and the mutual jealousies and quarrels of the local governors were perhaps not altogether displeasing to the home Government.[1]

In this way bands of Hittite mercenaries came to be settled in various parts of Palestine, even in the extreme south. The sons of Arzawaya, "the Arzawan," established themselves in the neighbourhood of Jerusalem, whose king, by the way, seems to bear a Mitannian name. The statement in the Book of Genesis that Heth was the son of Canaan receives a new signification from the Tel el-Amarna tablets.

But Hittite influence in Southern Palestine goes back to an earlier epoch than the age of the tablets. The painted pottery found in the "Amorite" strata of Lachish and Gezer shows remarkable affinities to the pottery discovered by Chantre at Boghaz Keui, and Mr. J. L. Myres has succeeded in tracing it in a fairly continuous line to the region north of the Halys.[2] Here was found the red ochre—or *sandaraké*, as it was called—which was used in the decoration of the pottery, and after the introduction of two other colours still remained the principal feature in the system of ornamentation. This Hittite or Cappadocian pottery was carried westward along the road which led from Boghaz Keui towards the Troad, and south-eastwards across the Taurus into Syria. It was probably the ultimate origin of the painted Minoan or "Kamâres" pottery of Krete.

[1] The facts were first stated in my article in the *Contemporary Review*, August 1905, pp. 264-77, which is reprinted as chapter vii. of the present book.

[2] *Journal of the Anthropological Institute*, 1903, xxxiii. pp. 367-400.

The introduction of Hittite pottery into Canaan where it tended to supersede the native ware, was doubtless the result of trade. But in ancient Asia the trader and the soldier were very apt to march side by side. The soldier opened the way for the trader and kept it for him, quite as much as the trader opened it for the soldier. Hence it is not surprising that the Assyrian monuments should furnish incidental evidence of the Hittite occupation of Palestine at an early date. In the inscriptions of Babylonia, as we have seen, Palestine and Syria are "the land of the Amorites"; the name went back to an immemorial antiquity, and indicates that at the time it was first given the Amorites were the ruling population in the West. But in the Assyrian inscriptions the place of the Amorites is taken by the Hittites. For the Assyrians, Syria is "the land of the Hittites," and in the later historical texts even the Israelites and Philistines are classed as "Hittite."[1]

Canaan, however, was already well known to the Assyrians in the age of the Tel el-Amarna correspondence, when the ambassadors of the Assyrian king carried letters and presents through it to the Pharaoh. It must, therefore, have been at a still earlier period that they first became acquainted with it, and at this period Hittite influence must have been so predominant as to cause them to discard the name of Amorite, consecrated though it was by the long-continued usage of Babylonian literature, and to employ instead of it the name of Hittite.

[1] By Shalmaneser II. (*Black Obelisk*, 61) and Sargon. Sennacherib describes his famous campaign against Phœnicia and Judah as made "to the land of the Hittites."

But it was in the direction of the Greek seas that Hittite influence was most powerful. Through Asia Minor Babylonian culture penetrated to the West. A native imitation of the Babylonian seal-cylinder was found by Dr. Schliemann in the ruins of Hissarlik,[1] and the so-called "heraldic" position of the lions at Mykenæ can be traced back through Asia Minor to the designs of the Babylonian gem-cutters. The winged horse, Pegasus, is found on Hittite seals, and, like the double-headed eagle of Eyuk and other composite figures, is derived from Babylonian proto-types.[2] They represented the first attempts of the creative power, as conceived of by Babylonian cosmology, and an old Babylonian legend of the creation accordingly describes the monsters suckled by Tiamât as "warriors with the bodies of birds, men with the faces of ravens."[3] The fantastic monsters of "Minoan" art, which have been brought to light by the excavations in Krete, claim an intimate connection with the similar composite beings which are a characteristic of Hittite art.[4]

The early Hittite art of Asia Minor, as I pointed out many years ago, is dependent on that of Babylonia,

[1] *Ilios*, p. 693. What seem to be similar characters on a seal-cylinder found in the copper-age cemetry of Agia Paraskevi in Cyprus have recently been published by me in the *Proceedings of the Society of Biblical Archæology*, June 1906, plate ii. No. xi. See above, p. 141.

[2] One of these seals, with the name of Tua-is, "the Charioteer," in Hittite hieroglyphs, is in the possession of M. de Clercq. Another is figured by Layard, *Culte de Mithra*, xliv. 3.

[3] See Sayce, *Religions of Ancient Egypt and Babylonia*, pp. 377–9.

[4] See Hogarth, "The Zakro Sealings," in the *Journal of Hellenic Studies*, xxii. pp. 76–93, and plates vi.–x.

and has little in common with the art of Assyria.[1] It is not until we come to the later Hittite monuments of Cilicia and Syria that the influence of Assyrian art makes itself visible. Hence was derived the partiality of the Hittite artist for the composite animals that adorn the seal-cylinders of Babylonia, and which consequently became known wherever the seal-cylinder and the literary culture it accompanied had made their way. As I have already stated, though Subari was an Assyrian province and Kara Eyuk an Assyrian colony, the form of the cuneiform script that was used in Cappadocia was of Babylonian origin.

The writing material of "Minoan" Krete, we now know, consisted of clay tablets. The fact is a proof that the influence of Babylonian culture had extended thus far. But it was an indirect influence only. Though the clay tablet was employed, the characters impressed upon it were the native Kretan. This in itself, however, demonstrates how strong the influence must have been, for the Kretan characters, whether hieroglyphic or linear, were less easy to inscribe on clay than the cuneiform. Krete, moreover, is a land of rock and stone rather than of clay. We may infer, therefore, from the use of the Babylonian material that the first impulse to write was inspired by the civilization of Babylonia.

How it was brought to Krete we do not know. It may have passed over from the shores of Canaan ; it may have come from Cyprus or Asia Minor. A seal-cylinder, which I have lately published, and which was found in the early copper-age cemetery of Agia

[1] *Transactions of the Society of Biblical Archæology*, 1881, vii. 2, p. 27.

Paraskevi in Cyprus, shows that the so-called Cypriote syllabary was already in use in the island at a remote date,[1] and this syllabary is closely connected with the linear characters of Krete. Inscriptions in the same form of script have been found on the site of Troy, and the pre-Israelitish pottery of Southern Palestine is marked with signs which seem to be derived from it. So, too, is certain Egyptian pottery of the age of the Eighteenth dynasty, and even of the age of the Twelfth.[2]

It is possible that Krete was the birthplace of the picture writing which developed into the linear script of Knossos and the Cypriote syllabary; it is possible that it was rather Cyprus. I do not think, as I once did, that it comes from Asia Minor, for Asia Minor had its own pictographic system, which we see represented in the Hittite inscriptions, and an increased knowledge of this system tends to dissociate it from the pictographs and syllabaries of Krete and Cyprus.

Wherever it arose, however, it was associated with the Babylonian writing material and the Babylonian seal-cylinder. So far as our present knowledge goes, Cyprus is more likely than any other part of the world to have been the meeting-point of Babylonian culture and the nascent civilization of the West. The numerous seal-cylinders which characterize the early copper age of the island are native imitations of Babylonian seal-cylinders of the epoch of Sargon of Akkad, when the boundaries of the

---

[1] See above, p. 141.

[2] Professor Petrie finds similar marks on Egyptian pottery of the prehistoric and early dynastic age ; see his table of signs in *The Royal Tombs of the First Dynasty* (Egypt Exploration Fund), i. p. 32.

Babylonian Empire were pushed to the coasts of the Mediterranean, if not into Cyprus itself, and the great eastern plain of Cyprus was better fitted to provide clay for the tablet than any other Mediterranean district with which I am acquainted.

That no written tablets have been found by the excavators in Cyprus is not surprising. In an island climate where heavy rains occur the unbaked tablet soon becomes hardly distinguishable from the earth in which it is embedded. It was almost by accident that even the practised eye of Dr. A. J. Evans was first led to notice the clay tablets of Knossos.

The Greek term δέλτος, which was borrowed from the language of Canaan, is evidence that the tablet was once known to the Greeks. For the letters of the Phœnician and Greek alphabet rolls of papyrus or leather were needed ; the fact that the writing material was a tablet and not a roll refers us back to Babylonia. With the introduction of the Phœnician letters the word δέλτος necessarily changed its meaning, and became synonymous with a wooden board. But it is possible that a reminiscence of its original signification is preserved in a famous passage of the *Iliad* (vi. 169), where the later " board " has been substituted for the earlier " tablet." Here we are told how Bellerophon carried with him to Lycia " baleful signs "—which may have been the pictographs of Krete or the Hittites, or even cuneiform characters— written upon " a folded board." The expression would have most naturally originated in the folded clay tablet of early Babylonia, the inner tablet being enclosed in an envelope on which the address or a description of the contents of the document is written.

On the literary side, however, this is the utmost contribution that we can claim for Babylonia to have made to historical Greece. In the sphere of religion it is possible that the anthropomorphism of Greece was influenced by the anthropomorphism of Babylonia through Asia Minor, where the rock sculptures of Boghaz Keui show how the primitive Hittite fetishes had become human deities like those of Chaldæa ; in the sphere of philosophy Thales and Anaximander clothed in a Greek dress the cosmological theories of the Babylonians ; and in the domain of art the heraldry and composite monsters of Babylonia made their way to Europe, while the Ionic artists of Ephesus carved ivories into forms so Oriental in character that similar figures found in the palace of Sargon have been pronounced to be the work of Phœnicians. But the literary culture of historical Greece did not begin until the tide of Babylonian influence had already rolled back from Western Asia, when the Phœnician alphabet had taken the place of the cuneiform syllabary in Syria, and the Hittite populations of Asia Minor had returned to their clumsy hieroglyphs.

It is, however, remarkable how very nearly the cuneiform script became what the Phœnician alphabet has been called, "the mother of the alphabets of the world." At one time it covered nearly the whole area of the civilized globe. A seal-cylinder with a cuneiform inscription in an unknown language has been discovered on the hills near Herat ;[1] in the west its

[1] *Journal of the Asiatic Society of Bengal*, xi. pp. 316 *sqq.* The cylinder was bought by Major Pottinger, but afterwards lost. The inscription seems to read : *AN Nin*(?)-*zi-in Su-lukh*(?)-

use extended as far as Cappadocia, perhaps further. Northward it made its home in Armenia ; southward it obliged even the Egyptian Foreign Office to employ it for correspondence, while military scribes wrote in it their memoranda of the Pharaoh's campaigns. In both Mitanni and Van the syllabary was on the high-road to becoming an alphabet; in Persia it actually became one.

But this final evolution came too late. A simpler script had already entered the field, and won its way in lands where clay was scarce and other writing materials more easily procurable. Indeed, it is probable that the presence or absence of clay suitable for writing purposes had quite as much to do with the spread of the cuneiform script as the political events which transformed the map of Western Asia. Canaan still continued to write in cuneiform characters after the empire of Babylonia had been exchanged for that of Egypt, while the use of the script never penetrated far into the limestone regions of the Mediterranean. It was probably the geological formation of Europe more than anything else which saved us to-day from having to learn the latest modification of the cursive writing of the Babylonian plain.

But it had been a potent instrument of civilization in its day, perhaps more potent even than the Phœnician alphabet, for its sway lasted for thousands of years. It was at once the symbol and the inspiring spirit of a culture whose roots go back to the very

---

me-am-el Khi-ti-sa ARAD-na—" To the god Nin(?)-zin, Sulukh-ammel (?) son of Khiti, his servant."

beginnings of human civilization, and to which we still owe part of our own heritage of civilized life. Babylonia was the mother-land of astronomy and irrigation; from thence a knowledge of copper seems to have spread through Western Asia; it was there that the laws and regulations of trade were first formulated, and the earliest legal code, so far as we know, was compiled. Babylonian theology and cosmology left their impress upon beliefs and views of the world which have passed through Judæa to Europe, and the astrology and magic which played so active a part in the mental history of the Middle Ages were Babylonian creations. It is not a little remarkable that an Etruscan model of the liver in bronze (discovered at Piacenza), divided and inscribed for the purposes of haruspicy, finds its counterpart and probably also its prototype in the clay copy of a liver, similarly divided and inscribed, which was found in Babylonia.[1] We are children of our fathers, and amongst our spiritual fathers must be reckoned the Babylonians.

[1] The Etruscan monument is described by Deecke, *Das Templum von Piacenza* (*Etruskische Forschungen*, iv. 1880) and *Etruskische Forschungen und Studien*, part ii. (1882). For the Babylonian prototype, see Boissier, *Note sur un Monument babylonien se rapportant à l'extispicine* (1899).

CHAPTER VII

CANAAN IN THE CENTURY BEFORE THE EXODUS

IT is now nearly twenty years ago since the archæological world was startled, not to say revolutionized, by the discovery of the cuneiform tablets of Tel el-Amarna in Upper Egypt. Nor was it the archæological world only which the discovery affected. The historian and the theologian have equally had to modify and forsake their old ideas and assumptions, and the criticism of the Old Testament writings has entered upon a new and altogether unexpected stage. The archæologist, the historian and the Biblical critic alike can never again return to the point of view which was dominant before 1887, or regard the ancient world of the East with the unbelieving eyes of a Grote or a Cornewall Lewis. A single archæological discovery has upset mountains of learned discussion, of ingenious theory and sceptical demonstration.

At the risk of repeating a well-worn tale, I will describe briefly the nature of the discovery. In the ruins of a city and palace which, like the palace of Aladdin, rose out of the desert sands into gorgeous magnificence for a short thirty years and then perished utterly, some 300 clay tablets were found, inscribed, not with the hieroglyphics of Egypt, but with the cuneiform characters of Babylonia. They were, in fact, the contents of the Foreign Office of Amon-hotep IV., the "Heretic King" of Egyptian history, who endeavoured to reform the old religion of Egypt and to substitute for it a pantheistic monotheism. This was about 1400 years before the birth of Christ, and a full century before the Israelitish Exodus. The attempt failed in spite of the fanatical efforts of its royal patron to force it upon his people, and of his introduction of religious persecution for the first time into the world. The Eighteenth dynasty, to which he belonged, and which had conquered Western Asia, went down in civil and religious war; the Asiatic Empire of Egypt was lost, and a new dynasty sat on the throne of Thebes.

The archives in the Foreign Office included not only the foreign correspondence of Amon-hotep's own reign, but the foreign correspondence also of his father, which he had carried with him from Thebes when he founded his new capital at Tel el-Amarna. And the scope and character of it are astounding. There are letters from the kings of Babylonia and Assyria, of Mesopotamia and the Hittites, of Cilicia and Cappadocia, besides letters and communications of all sorts from the Egyptian governors and vassal princes in Canaan and Syria. Most of the correspondence is in the language of Babylonia; it is only in a few rare instances that the cuneiform characters embody the actual language of the people from whom the letters were sent. It is difficult to imagine anything more subversive of the ideas about the ancient history of the East, which were current twenty years ago, than the conclusions to be drawn from this correspondence. It proved that, so far as literary culture is concerned, the civilized Oriental world in the Mosaic age was quite as civilized as our own. There were schools and libraries all over it, in which a foreign language and a complicated foreign system of writing formed an essential part of education. It proved that this education was widely spread : there are letters from Bedâwîn shêkhs as well as from a lady who was much interested in politics. It showed that this correspondence was active and regular, that those who took part in it wrote to each other on the trivial topics of the day, and that the high-roads and postal service were alike well organized. We learned that the nations of the Orient were no isolated units cut off from one another except when one of them made war with the other, but that, on the contrary, their mutual relations were as close and intimate as those of modern Europe. The Babylonian king in his distant capital on the Euphrates sent to condole with the Egyptian Pharaoh on his father's death like a modern potentate, and was every whit as anxious to protect and encourage the trade of his country as Mr. Chamberlain. Indeed, the privileges of the merchant and the sacredness of his person had long been a matter of international law.

In one respect the advocates of international harmony and arbitration were better off in the Mosaic age than they are in the Europe of to-day. There was no difficulty about diversities of language and the danger of being misunderstood. The language of diplomacy, of education and trade was everywhere the same, and was understood, read and written by all educated persons. Even the Egyptian lord of Western Asia had to swallow his pride and write in the language and script of Babylonia when he corresponded with his own subjects in Canaan. Indeed, like English officials in Egypt, who are supposed to write to one another on official business in French, his own Egyptian envoys and commissioners sent their official communications in the foreign tongue. The Oriental world in the century before the Exodus thus anticipated the Roman Empire.

Canaan was the centre and focus of the correspondence. It was the battle-ground and meeting-place of the great powers of the Eastern world. It had long been a province of Babylonia, and, like the rest of the Babylonian Empire, subject to Babylonian law and permeated by Babylonian literary culture. It was during these centuries of Babylonian government that it had come to adopt as its own the script and language of its rulers ; the deities of Babylonia were worshipped on the high places of Palestine, and Babylonian legends and traditions were taught in its schools.

Out of Canaan had marched the Hyksos who conquered Egypt. The names of their kings found on the monuments that have survived to us are distinctively Canaanite of the patriarchal period ; among them is Jacob-el, or Jacob, whom the Alexandrine Jews seem to have identified with their own ancestor. While the Hyksos Pharaohs reigned, Egypt was but a dependency of Canaan ; the source of Hyksos power lay in Canaan, and their Egyptian capital was accordingly placed close to the Canaanitish frontier.

When, after five generations of warfare, the native princes of Thebes succeeded at last in expelling the Hyksos conquerors from the valley of the Nile and in founding the Eighteenth dynasty, they perceived that their best hope of preventing a second Asiatic conquest lay in possessing themselves of the land which was, as it were, the key to their own. The Hyksos conquest, in fact, had shown that Canaan was at once a link between Asia and Africa, and the open gate which let the invader into the fertile fields of Egypt. The war, therefore, that had ended by driving the Asiatic out of Egypt was now carried into his own home. Campaign after campaign finally crushed Canaanitish resistance, and the Egyptian standards were planted on the banks of the Euphrates. Palestine and Syria were transformed into Egyptian provinces ; in the language of the tenth chapter of Genesis, they became the brothers of Mizraim.

The Tel el-Amarna letters tell us how the new provinces were organized. The most important cities were placed under Egyptian governors, many of whom, however, were natives. But they were carefully watched by Egyptian commissioners, to whom the control of the military forces was entrusted, as well as by special high-commissioners sent from time to time by the imperial Government. Local jealousies and rivalries, moreover, among the governors prevented union among them against the central power, and up to a certain point were not discouraged by the Egyptian Foreign Office. The Tel el-Amarna letters offer us a curious picture of the extent to which their mutual animosities were carried in the days when the Egyptian Empire was growing feeble. All the governors protest their devotion to the court, and all like are accused by their rivals of intriguing and even fighting against it.

Besides the states which were thus directly under Egyptian rule, there were also protected states. Here the representative of the old line of kings was allowed to retain a titular authority, though in reality his power was not greater than that of the governors in other states. But, whether governor or protected prince his duty to the imperial Government was clearly marked out for him. He had to levy the taxes and send a fixed amount of tribute to the Egyptian Treasury, to provide a certain number of militia, and to send official reports to the king. He had further to see that the troops of the army of occupation were duly provided with pay and maintenance.

The army of occupation in the reign of Amonhotep IV. does not seem to have been large. The imperial forces were needed at home to enforce the new faith upon the Egyptian people, and to put down the discontent that was growing there. We hear, however, of "the household troops," who belonged to the standing army of Egypt and formed the nucleus of the permanent garrison. How many of them were native Egyptians it is impossible to say; as we hear of Kushites or Ethiopians among them, it is probable that the Sudanese were at least as largely employed on foreign service as the Egyptians themselves. The Egyptian has never been fond of military service, whereas, we all now know, the Sudanese is essentially a fighting animal.

Both sides of the Jordan were included in the Egyptian administration. One of the Tel el-Amarna letters, for example, is from a governor of "the field of Bashan." It is characteristic of the whole series, and shows what the relations were between the army of occupation and the native levies. I cannot do better than quote it in full: " To the king, my lord, thus says Artamanya, the governor of the Field of Bashan, thy servant: at the feet of the king, my lord, seven times seven do I fall. Behold, thou hast written to me to join the household troops, and how could I be a dog (of the king) and not go? Behold, I and my soldiers and my chariots will join the household troops in whatever place the king my lord orders."

The name of Artamanya is not Semitic; neither is it Egyptian. The fact brings us to one of the most interesting and unexpected results of the decipherment of the Tel el-Amarna correspondence. And this is that the ruling caste in the Palestine of the Mosaic age was largely of Hittite origin, or had come from those countries of the north whose population was related in blood and language to the Hittites of Asia Minor.

In Northern Mesopotamia was a kingdom which ranked with those of Egypt and Babylonia as regarded power and influence. Its native name was Mitanni; the Hebrews, like the Egyptians, called it the kingdom of Aram Naharaim. It stretched from Assyria to the Orontes, and contended with the Hittites of Carchemish for the possession of the fords of the Euphrates. Its ruler, had descended upon it from the highlands of Armenia and the Caucasus, and had reduced the native Aramæan population to servitude. There are frequent references in the Tel el-Amarna tablets to Mitannian intrigues in Canaan. Mitannian armies had from time to time marched against the Canaanitish cities, and although there was now a nominal alliance between

N

Mitanni and Egypt, and the royal families of the two countries were united by marriage, the Mitannian court never lost an opportunity of sending secret support to the disaffected princes of Canaan or of encouraging them in their revolts from the Egyptian Government. In many parts of the country the ruling family continued to be Mitannian, and accordingly we find more than one governor who bears a Mitannian name. Thus one of them, as we see, was governor of Bashan, and there was another who had his seat near the Sea of Galilee.

Mitannian influence, however, was chiefly confined to the northern part of Palestine. It was otherwise with the Hittites, whose marauding bands penetrated as far south as the frontiers of Egypt. The important part they played in the early history of Canaan and the substantial element they must have contributed to the future population of the country has but lately been disclosed to us by the advance that has been made in the interpretation of the Tel el-Amarna texts. We have at last obtained an explanation of the fact that whereas in the older Babylonian period Canaan was known as "the land of the Amorites," it was called by the Assyrians "the land of the Hittites." The Assyrian kings even speak of Judah and Moab as "Hittite," and the town of Ashdod is described by Sargon as a "Hittite" state. What this must mean has indeed long been recognized by the Assyriologists. When the Assyrians first became acquainted with Palestine the Hittites must have been there the dominant power. But how and when this came about we have but just begun to learn, and it is the story of the Hittite occupation of Canaan, as a better knowledge of the Tel el-Amarna tablets is making possible, that I now propose to describe.

The Hittite race was of Cappadocian origin. Professor Ramsay has pointed out that the hieroglyphic characters which they used in their inscriptions must have been invented on the treeless plateau of Central Asia Minor, and that their capital, whose ruins now strew the ground at Boghaz Keui, north of the Halys, was the centre towards which all the early high-roads of Asia Minor converge. But they extended on both sides of the Taurus Mountains, and at an early date had planted themselves in Northern Syria. I have lately succeeded in deciphering their inscriptions, which have so long baffled our attempts to read them, and one result of my decipherment is the discovery of an unexpected fact. I find that the name of Hittite was confined to that portion of the race which lived eastward and southward of the Taurus. In Asia Minor itself, their first cradle and home, they called themselves Kas or Kasians ; it was the kingdom of Kas over which the Hittite lords of Boghaz Keui claimed to rule, and it is still as kings of Kas that they are entitled on the monuments of Carchemish, though here they also acknowledge the name of Hittite.

The name of Kas is met with in the Tel el-Amarna tablets, where it has hitherto been misunderstood. The kings of the Hittites, of Mitanni and of Kas are associated together as supporting the enemies of the Egyptian Pharaoh or attacking his cities in Syria. Hitherto we have supposed that Kas signified Babylonia, though the supposition had but little in its favour, and a different name is given to Babylonia in passages where there is no doubt as to what country is meant. Now, however, all becomes clear: in the age of the tablets there were still four Hittite kingdoms in the north : Kas in Asia Minor, the Hittites proper, east and south of the Taurus, Mitanni in Mesopotamia, and Naharaim on the Orontes. Shortly afterwards they were all swallowed up in the empire of the "great king" of the Hittites, whose southern capital was at Kadesh. Some Kasians had found their way to Jerusalem, where the king Ebed-Kheba —whose name is compounded with that of a Mitannian deity—writes to the Egyptian Government to excuse his conduct in regard to them. They had been accused of plundering the Pharaoh's territory and murdering his servants ; he assures the court that nothing of the sort is true. They are still in his house, where it would seem they formed his bodyguard. But, on the other hand, there were other Hittites in the neighbourhood of Jerusalem who were really enemies to the king and threatened Jerusalem itself. These he calls Khabiri, or "Confederates," a name in which, despite history and probability, certain writers have insisted upon seeing the Hebrews of the Old Testament. But Dr. Knudtzon's fresh collation of the Tel el-Amarna texts has at last dispelled the mystery. The Khabiri turn out to have been bands of Hittite condottieri, who sold their military services to the highest bidder and carved out principalities for themselves in the south of Canaan. The Egyptian Government found them useful in escorting and protecting the trading caravans to Asia Minor and the Taurus region, and as long as their leaders professed themselves the devoted servants of the

Pharaoh it was quite willing to overlook such little accidents as their capture and sack of a Canaanitish town or the murder of a Canaanitish prince.

One of these Hittite leaders, Aita-gama by name, had possessed himself of the city of Kadesh on the Orontes, which in the following century was to become the capital of a Hittite empire. In a letter to the Egyptian court he has the audacity to assert that he was merely claiming his patrimony, the whole district having belonged to his father. If there is any truth in this it can only mean that his father had already led a troop of Hittite raiders into this portion of the Egyptian territory.

Along with Aita-gama two other Hittite chieftains had marched, Teuwatti, whose name appears in the native texts under the form of Tuates, and Arzawaya. Arzawaya means "a man of Arzawa," the country whose language has been revealed to us in one of the Tel el-Amarna letters, and which proves to be the same as the Hittite dialect found in the cuneiform tablets of Boghaz Keui. We are told that he came from a city which was in the neighbourhood of the Karmalas, in Southern Cappadocia. Arzawaya helped Teuwatti to conquer Damascus and then led his followers further south. Here he acted as a free-lance, hiring himself and his mercenaries to the rival Canaanitish princes and professing himself to be all the while a faithful servant of the Egyptian king. It is amusing to read one of his letters to the Egyptian court: "To my lord the king thus writes Arzawaya, of Rukhiza. At the feet of my lord I prostrate myself. My lord the king wrote that I should join the household troops of the king my lord and his numerous officers." Here follow four words of Hittite which are accompanied by the translation: "I am a servant of the king my lord." Then the letter proceeds: "I will join the household troops of the king my lord and his officers; and I will send everything after them and march wherever there is rebellion against the king my lord. And we will deliver his enemies into the hand of the king our lord." Doubtless Arzawaya expected to be well paid for his help.

There is another letter from Arzawaya to the Pharaoh in which he calls himself "the dust of his feet and the ground on which he treads." But in this letter he has to explain away the share he took in entering the town of Gezer along with Labbawa,[1] another Hittite leader, and there infringing the royal prerogative by summoning a levy of the militia. In the eyes of the home Government this was a much more serious matter than merely plundering or killing a few of its Canaanitish subjects, as it was equivalent to usurping the functions of the imperial power.

Labbawa also had to write and ask for forgiveness, and assure the Pharaoh that he is his "devoted slave," who does "not withhold his tribute" or disobey the "requests" of the Egyptian commissioners. In fact, he concludes his letter with declaring that "if the king should write to me: Run a sword of bronze into your heart and die, I would not fail to execute the king's command." All the same, however, he had established himself securely on Mount Shechem, from whence, like Joshua in after days, he was able to make raids on the surrounding Canaanitish towns.

---

[1] Labbawa, or Labawa, is written Labbaya in the letter which is in the Arzawan language.

In the north we hear of him at Shunem and Gath-Rimmon, where he first appeared upon the scene in the train of the Egyptian army at a time when Amon-hotep III. was suppressing an insurrection in that part of Palestine. It is probable that he had just arrived with his band of condottieri, attracted by the pay and the chance of plunder that the Egyptian Pharaoh offered the free-lance. By a curious fatality it was also in this same locality that he afterwards met his death at the hands of the people of Gina—the Cana of Galilee, probably, of St. John's Gospel.

Labbawa cast envious eyes on the important city of Megiddo, and its governor—who, by the way, is mentioned in one of the cuneiform tablets found three years ago by the Austrian excavators on the site of Taanach—sent piteous appeals for assistance against him to the Egyptian Government. The beleaguered governor declared that so closely invested was he by the Hittite free-lances that he could not venture outside the gates of his town. The peasantry were afraid even to bring vegetables into it, and unless help were forthcoming from Egypt, Megiddo was doomed. After all, however, Labbawa was not only unable to possess himself of the Canaanitish stronghold, but was taken prisoner and confined in the very place he had hoped to capture. But fortune befriended him. He managed to bribe the governor of Acre, and the latter, on the pretext that he was going to send Labbawa by sea to Egypt, took him out of prison and set him free.

Labbawa now turned his attention to the south of Palestine—the future territory of Judah. Here he entered into alliance with the king of Jerusalem, or, to speak more precisely, was taken into his pay, and the two together waged war on the neighbouring states. One of the Egyptian governors complains that they had robbed him of Keilah, and he had to wait for Labbawa's death before he could recover his city.

One of the two letters in the Tel el-Amarna collection which are in the Arzawan or Hittite language was written by Labbawa, as we have lately learned from Dr. Knudtzon's revised copy of it. In this he calls himself a native of the Hittite district of Uan, near Aleppo, and refers to "the Hittite king," though our knowledge of the language is too imperfect to allow us to understand the meaning of the reference. The letter is addressed simply "to my lord," and we do not know, therefore, whether it was intended for Hittite or Egyptian eyes. After his settlement in Palestine, however, Labbawa adopted the official language of the country; his letters to the Pharaoh are in Babylonian, and his son bore the characteristically Semitic name of Mut-Baal. The fact is an interesting example of the rapid way in which the Hittite settlers in Palestine were Semitized. They brought no women with them, and their wives accordingly were natives of Canaan.

Labbawa left two sons behind him, who, in spite of their Semitic education, followed in their father's footsteps and continued to lead his company of Hittite mercenaries. Mut-Baal, moreover, made himself useful to the Government by escorting the trading caravans to Cappadocia, a fact which proves that he still maintained relations with the country of his origin. The alliance between Ebed-Kheba of Jerusalem and his father, however, had come to an end ; Ebed-Kheba now had the Hittites of Kas in his pay, and no longer needed the services of the sons of Labbawa. They therefore transferred themselves to his rivals, together with the sons of Arzawaya, who, like Labbawa, was now dead, and Ebed-Kheba soon found himself in difficulties. The result was letter after letter from him to the Egyptian court, begging for help against his enemies, and declaring that if no help came the king's territory would be lost. These appeals seem to have met with no response; the Egyptian Government was by no means assured of Ebed-Kheba's loyalty, and knew that if the territory of Jerusalem were to pass into the hands of the Hittite chieftain it would make but little difference to the imperial power. The tribute would still be paid, the Egyptian commissioner would still be respected, and the new rulers of the district would profess themselves the faithful subjects of the Pharaoh. There would merely be a change of governors, and nothing more. The Hittite mercenaries were formidable only in the petty struggles which took place between the rival Canaanitish governors; when it came to dealing with the regular army of Egypt they were numerically too few to be of account.

Ebed-Kheba calls the followers of Labbawa and Arzawaya "Khabiri." I have long ago pointed out that the word is found elsewhere in the Assyrian texts in the sense of " Confederates," and that its identification with the Hebrews of the Old Testament, though phonetically possible, is historically impossible. Now that we know the nationality of Labbawa and Arzawaya the question is finally settled, and we can explain a hitherto puzzling passage in one of Ebed-Kheba's letters, in which he says that "when ships were on the sea the arm of the mighty king seized Naharaim and Kas, but now the Khabiri have seized the cities of the king." Naharaim lay southward of the gulf of Antioch, while Kas extended to the Cilician coast, and they were thus, both of them, within reach of a maritime Power; they were, moreover, both of them Hittite regions, Naharaim being the district afterwards called Khattinâ, "the Hittite land," by the Assyrians, while Kas was the Hittite kingdom of Cappadocia. Ebed-Kheba, therefore, is drawing a comparison between the power of "the mighty king" in the days when an Egyptian fleet controlled the sea and the present time when Hittite marauders are seizing without let or hindrance the king's cities on the very borders of Egypt. Even Lachish and Ashkelon had joined the enemy.

Perhaps the most important of the King of Jerusalem's letters is one which has hitherto been misunderstood, partly owing to its being broken in half and the relation of the two halves to one another not being recognized, partly to the imperfections of the published copy. Now that a complete and accurate text of it lies before us, its meaning has ceased to be a riddle, and I will therefore give here the first translation that has been made of the completed text—

"To the king my lord thus says Ebed-Kheba thy servant: at the feet of my lord the king seven times seven I prostrate myself. Behold, Malchiel has not separated himself from the sons of Labbawa and the sons of Arzawaya so as to claim the king's land for them. A governor who commits such an act, why

has not the king questioned him (about it)?   Behold,
Malchiel and Tagi have committed such an act by
seizing the city of Rabbah.   And now as to Jerusalem,
if this land belongs to the king, why is it that Gaza has
been appointed for the (residence of the) king ('s
commissioner)?   Behold the land of Gath-Carmel is
in the power of Tagi, and the men of Gath are (his)
bodyguard.   He is (now) in Beth-Sannah.   But (nevertheless) we will act.   Malchiel wrote to Tagi that
they should give Labbawa and Mount Shechem to
the district of the Khabiri, and he took some boys as
slaves.   They granted all their demands to the people
of Keilah.   But we will rescue Jerusalem.   The garrison which you sent by Khaya the son of Meri-Ra
has been taken by Hadad-mikhir and stationed in his
house at Gaza.   [I have sent messengers] to Egypt,
[and may] the king [listen to me]. . . . There is no
garrison of the king [here].   Verily by the life of the
king Pa-ur has gone down to Egypt; he has left me
and is in Gaza.   But let the king entrust to him a
garrison for the defence of the land.   All the land of
the king has revolted.   Send Yenkhamu and let him
take charge of the king's land.

"(Postscript): To the secretary of the king says
Ebed-Kheba your servant: [bring] what I say
clearly before the king.   Kindest regards to you!
I am your servant."

The references in this letter are explained in other
letters from the same correspondent.   Malchiel was
the native governor of the Hebron district, and had
married the daughter of Tagi, whose name does not
sound Semitic.   The Hittite mercenaries of Labbawa
from Shechem and of Arzawaya, who does not seem

to have established himself in any special district of
the country, were now in the pay of Malchiel, while
Ebed-Kheba, as we have seen, had secured the
services of another body of Hittites from Kas. He
had been accused at the Egyptian court of seeking by
their means to make himself independent, and more
than one of his letters is occupied with defending
himself and bringing a counter-charge against Malchiel. Malchiel, however, secured the support of the
royal commissioner, Yenkhamu, who agreed to his
employment of the Hittite condottieri. With their
assistance Keilah had been recovered from the hands
of Ebed-Kheba, who, at an earlier date, had got Labbawa to seize it for him, but after Labbawa's death
the tables were turned, and his sons had offered their
services to the rival party, doubtless for the sake of
better pay. It was now that Malchiel summoned the
militia of Gezer, Gath-Carmel and Keilah, and made
himself master of Rabbah, a small place north-west of
Keilah and Hebron, which Ebed-Kheba asserted
belonged to *his* territory. The tide was beginning to
turn against the King of Jerusalem: his enemies were
in greater favour at court than he was himself, and
they had the support of the Hittite bands. It was in
vain that he appealed to the Egyptian Government
for aid and declared that not only had his rivals
given Mount Shechem to the Hittite free-lances, but
that by their action against himself they were de-
livering the whole of Southern Palestine into Hittite
hands. "The king," he writes, "no longer has any
territory, the Khabiri have wasted all the lands of the
king. If the royal troops come this year, the
country will remain my lord the king's, but if no

troops come, the territory of the king my lord is lost."

At this point the story breaks off abruptly. The Tel el-Amarna correspondence comes to an end and the fate of Jerusalem and the surrounding districts is unknown to us. Soon afterwards religious troubles at home forced the Egyptian Government to withdraw its troops from Canaan altogether, and for awhile the Egyptian empire in Asia ceased to exist. It was restored, however, by Seti I. and his son, Ramses II., at the beginning of the Nineteenth dynasty, and among the cities whose conquest is celebrated by Ramses on the walls of the Ramesseum at Thebes is Shalem or Jerusalem. But this second Egyptian empire in Asia did not last long, and when the Israelitish Exodus took place it was already passing away. When some years later the Israelitish invaders planted themselves in Labbawa's old stronghold on Mount Shechem, the Egyptian occupation of Canaan belonged to the history of the past.

Like the Saxons in England, however, the Hittite chieftains must have founded principalities for themselves in the south of Canaan, as we know from the evidence of the Tel el-Amarna tablets and the Egyptian monuments that they did in the north. Ezekiel, in fact, tells us that the mother of Jerusalem was a Hittite, and the Jebusites, from whom Jerusalem took its name in the age of the Israelitish conquest, were probably the descendants of the followers of the Hittite Arzawaya. They had, moreover, found a Hittite population already settled in the country, descendants of older bands who had made their way from the highlands of Asia Minor to the frontiers of Egypt in days when as yet Abraham was unborn. At the very commencement of the Egyptian twelfth dynasty we hear of the Pharaohs destroying "the palaces of the Hittites" in Southern Palestine,[1] and archæology has recently shown that the painted pottery discovered in the earlier strata of Lachish and Gezer by English excavators had its original home in Northern Cappadocia and is an enduring evidence of Hittite culture and trade.

The Hittites had been preceded in their occupation of Canaan by the Amorites, as we have learnt from the Babylonian inscriptions.   But in the Tel el-Amarna age the specifically Amoritish territory was in the north, eastward of Tyre and Gebal.   Here Ebed-Asherah and his son Aziru had their seat, and from hence they led their forces northwards towards Aleppo to resist "the king of the Hittites" on behalf of the Egyptian Government, or attacked the Phœnician cities on their own account.   In the north, in fact, they played much the same part as the Hittite mercenaries did in the south, with the additional advantage of being able to secure secret assistance when it was needed from Mitanni.   Between Amorites and Hittites the Canaanites must have had a somewhat unhappy time, like the Britons after the departure of the Roman legions, who found themselves

---

[1] A copy of the text (Louvre, C I) is given by Professor Breasted in the *American Journal of Semitic Languages and Literature*, xxi. 3 (1905).   The determinative attached to the name is not that of "country" but of "going," showing that the scribe supposed the name to be connected with some otherwise unknown word that signified "to go," just as in Gen. xxiii. "The sons of Heth" are supposed by the Hebrew writer to derive their name from the Hebrew *khath*, "terror."

the alternate prey of Saxons and Scots. But we can now understand and appreciate the ethnological notice in the Book of Numbers (xiii. 29), which tells us that "the Hittites and the Jebusites and the Amorites dwell in the mountains, and the Canaanites dwell by the sea and by the coast of Jordan."

The Amorite princes, however, were more formidable to the Egyptian Government than the Hittite chieftains, or else must have played their cards a little too openly, for we find Aziru receiving a scolding such as the Egyptian court seldom had the courage or energy to give. The letter from the Egyptian Foreign Office, which is a long one, is worth translating in full—

"To the governor of the land of the Amorites [thus] says the king your lord. The governor of Gebal, thy brother, whom his brother has driven from the gate (of the city) has said: 'Take me and bring me back into my city, [and] I will then give you money, [for] I have nothing [of value] with me now.' So he spoke to you.

"Behold, you write to the king your lord saying: I am your servant like all the loyal governors who are each in his city. Yet you have acted wrongly in taking a governor whom his brother had driven from the gate of his city, and being in Sidon you handed him over to the governors (there) at your own discretion, as if you did not know that they were rebellious.

"If you are really a servant of the king why have you not seen that he should go up to the presence of the king your lord instead of thinking, 'This governor wrote to me saying, "Take me to thyself and restore me to my city"'?

"But if you have acted loyally and nothing that I write is correct, the king has devised a lie in saying that nothing which you declare is true.

"But it happens that one has heard that you have made a treaty with the (Hittite) prince of Kadesh to deliver food and drink to one another, and it is true. Why have you acted thus? Why have you made a treaty with a governor with whom another governor is at enmity? For if you act with loyalty to him and observe your and his engagements you cannot look after (our) interests as you have undertaken to do long ago. Whatever be your conduct in the matter you are not on the side of the king your lord.

"Now as for these men to whom you want to turn, they are seeking to get you into the fire and to burn (you) and all you most love. Whereas if you submit yourself to the king your lord, what is there which the king cannot do for you? If in anything you love to act wickedly and if you lay up wickedness, even thoughts of rebellion, in your heart, then you will die by the axe of the king along with all your family. Submit therefore to the king your lord, and you shall live, for you know that the king has no wish to be angry with all the land of Canaan.

"And since you write: 'Let the king excuse me this year and I will go next year to the court of the king my lord, my son not being with me,' the king your lord accordingly will excuse you this year as you have asked. Go yourself instead of sending your son, and you shall see the king in the sight of whom all the world lives, and do not say: let me be excused this year also from going to the court of the king

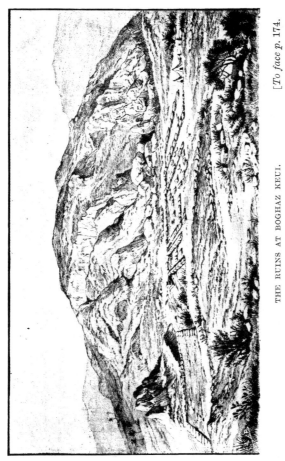

THE RUINS AT BOGHAZ KEUI.

[To face p. 174.

ONE OF THE PROCESSIONS IN THE RAVINE OF BOGHAZ.
(*See p.* 174).

HEAD OF ONE OF THE STATUES FROM
TELLO.

[*See p.* 73.

VASE OF SILVER, DEDICATED
TO NINGIRSU, BY ENTENA
PATESI OF LAGAS.

[*See p.* 58.

REVERSE OF A TABLET IN THE HITTITE LANGUAGE FROM
BOGHAZ KEUI.

[See Preface, p. vi.

your lord ; and do not send your son to the king your lord ; he must not go in your place.

" And now the king your lord has heard that you wrote to the king saying, ' Let the king my lord permit Khanni the messenger of the king to come to me for the second time, and I will deliver the enemies of the king into his hand.' Now he will go to you as you have asked ; do you therefore deliver them (to him) and do not let a single one of them escape. Now the king your lord sends you the names of the king's enemies in this letter by the hand of Khanni the king's messenger ; so deliver them to the king your lord and let not a single one of them escape, but put fetters of bronze upon their feet. Behold, the men you are to send to the king your lord are Sarru with all his sons, Tuia, Liya with all his sons, Yisyari with all his sons, (and) the son-in-law of Manya with his sons and wives. The treasurer of Khanni is the official who will read the dispatch. Dâsirtî, Pâlûwa and Nimmakhî have gone [to collect taxes ?] into the country of the Amorites.

" And know that the king, the Sun-god in heaven, is well ; his soldiers and chariots are many ; from the upper country to the lower country, from the rising of the sun [to] the setting of the sun all is peace."

We hear again of one of the rebels mentioned in this letter in the tablet discovered at Lachish in Palestine by Mr. Bliss. Yisyari is there described as inciting the governor of Lachish to revolt and promising assistance if he would call out the militia of his city against the king. That an Amorite of the north should thus have been able to interfere in the politics of a city in the south of Palestine is an interesting illustration of what I may call the solidarity of Syria and Canaan in the pre-Mosaic period. They had not yet been broken up into a series of isolated States ; like the Hittites, the Amorites still claimed to be a power in the future territory of Judah as well as in the neighbourhood of Sidon or Hamath.

It is possible that a well-known but somewhat mysterious personage of the Old Testament was one of the Hittite leaders who succeeded in carving out a principality for himself : I mean Balaam the son of Beor. He is said to have come from the Hittite town of Pethor near Carchemish, and besides being a seer and a prophet he was also a soldier who fell in the ranks of the Midianites in a war against Israel. But Balaam the son of Beor was not only a native of Pethor ; we hear of him again in the Book of Genesis, and here he appears as the first king of Edom, his name heading the list of Edomite kings extracted from the state annals of Edom and probably brought to Jerusalem when David conquered the country. In the light of what we have learnt from the tablets of Tel el-Amarna it is perhaps not going too far to suppose that in Balaam we have one of those Hittite chieftains who, after playing the part of prophet, made himself leader of a band of Hittite free-lances and established a kingdom for himself in Edom, finally falling in battle by the side of his Midianite allies.

However this may be, the important place occupied by the Hittites in creating the Canaan which the Israelites invaded is now clear. While the larger bands of Hittite raiders settled in the north, where they prepared the way for the Hittite king himself with his regular army, and where Hittite power became so firmly established that even the great Ramses could not dislodge it, smaller companies of condottieri made their way to the extreme south of Palestine, hiring their services to the rival governors and princes and seizing a town or district for themselves when the opportunity offered. So long as the tribute was paid, and its subjects were not too troublesome, the Egyptian Government looked on with equanimity while the states of Canaan were practically ruled by the leaders of foreign mercenaries who transferred their services from one paymaster to another with the most perfect impartiality.

What is most curious is that the Imperial Government recognized the legal position not only of the Hittite or Amorite mercenaries, but even of organized bands of Bedâwîn and outlaws. As for the Bedâwîn, it had companies of them in its own pay, like the Egyptian Government in more recent times, and the governor of Gebal complains that the Egyptian commissioner Pa-Hor had sent some of the latter to murder his garrison of Serdani or Sardinians, who were themselves mercenaries in the Egyptian army. That bodies of outlaws should have been subsidized by the native princes with the permission, or at least the connivance, of the Egyptian court may seem surprising. But after all it is only what we find happening in later times when the king of Gath similarly enrolled David and his band of outlaws into his bodyguard without any remonstrance on the part of the other Philistine "lords." Still it is startling to find one of the Pharaoh's governors coolly announcing that he and his soldiers and chariots, together with his brothers, his "cut-throats" and his Bedâwîn, are ready to join the royal troops, at the very time when another governor is piteously begging the great king to "save" him "out of the hands of the cut-throats and Bedâwîn." Here is a strange picture of Canaanitish life in the days when as yet the Israelite was not in the land.

The fact is, the Canaanites were an unwarlike people. Inland, they were agriculturists; on the sea coast they were traders. And, like other trading communities, they were disinclined to fight, preferring to entrust the protection of themselves and their property to a paid soldiery, while at the same time their wealth made them a tempting prize to the assailant. It is true that they maintained a native militia, as we have learned from one of the cuneiform tablets discovered at Taanach, but it was upon a small scale, and apparently so long as the person on the roll could produce the one or two men for whom he was responsible he was not himself obliged to serve. It was again a case of paying others to fight instead of themselves.

The fighting population of Canaan, in short, were the foreigners, and these it was who gradually made themselves its practical masters. The leaders of the mercenaries became the rulers of the Canaanite states, which thus passed into the hands of a dominant military caste. When the Israelites entered the country it was with this military upper class that they had principally to deal; where the Canaanite had not its protection he trusted for his defence to his iron chariots and the strong and lofty walls of his towns. It is instructive to read the long list of unconquered cities and districts given by the Hebrew historian in the first chapter of the Book of Judges; among them are the Jebusites of Jerusalem, while we are told that "the Amorites forced the children of Dan into the mountain, for they would not suffer them to come down to the valley."

Canaan, it will probably be thought, was a somewhat insecure country in which to live in the days of the Egyptian Empire. There seem to have been constant turmoil and confusion, governor attacking governor and bribing bands of foreign mercenaries to help him. But the turmoil and confusion were mainly on the surface. When a town is taken from one governor by another we do not hear of its population or their possessions suffering materially; they soon appear upon the scene again as prosperous as before. It is merely the governor and his immediate surroundings who suffer; the capture of the town was probably an affair amicably arranged between the condottieri who were attacking it and the condottieri who were its defenders. The Egyptian commissioners go up and down the country, hearing complaints and settling disputes, and no one ventures even to protest against their decisions, while a few Egyptian troops are stationed in places where the Government was not quite sure of the fidelity of its subjects. Caravans of merchants passed through Canaan going from Egypt to the north, and the traders of Babylonia and Asia Minor travelled along its high roads under the escort of Hittite and other chieftains who were subsidized for the purpose by the Egyptian court. Even in the days when the Egyptian Government was breaking up, the constant fighting among the foreign mercenaries and their employers seems to have affected the mass of the population little, if at all.

What happened when the strong hand and controlling power of the Egyptian Pharaoh were removed we do not yet know. We must look for information to the systematic excavations that are at last being made on the sites of the old Canaanitish towns. Already cuneiform tablets have been found on them, and though these belong to the Egyptian period we may hope that before long others may be discovered of later date. We have still to bridge over the age which elapsed between the final withdrawal of Egyptian domination and the conquest of the country by Philistines and Israelites. When that age begins the script and official language of Canaan are still Babylonian; when it closes the cuneiform characters have been superseded by the letters of the Phœnician alphabet, and the language of the inscriptions engraved in them is the language no longer of Babylonia or of Hittite lands, but of Canaan itself.

INDEX

Euphrates, 81, 102, 103
Evans, A. J., 141, 159, 183

Fibula, introduction of, 65, 66
Figurines in Elam, 52, 54; at Kara Eyuk, 171
Flower, Samuel, 8

Garstang, 62
Gezer, 57, 60, 63, 65, 145, etc., 154, 158, 198, 204, 206; graves at, 151
Gladstone, Dr., analysis of metals, 60, 61, 170
Gold, word for, 58
Gordium, pottery of, 171
Grotefend, 10–13, 17, 35
Gudea, 53, 59, 73, 141
Guyard, Stanislas, 33, 162

Hadad-nirari I., 57, 157, 172
Halévy, 28
Hall, H. R., 40
Hamadan, inscription of, 15
Hathor identified with Istar, 129
Haupt, 29
Haynes, 56
Hazael, 21
Hebrew, 142
Hebron, 203
Heeren, 13
Heraldic position in art, 117, 180
Herat, seal-cylinder from, 184
Herbert, Thomas, 9
Herodotus, 131
Heuzey, 40, 53, 117, 121, 133
Hezekiah, 21
Hierakonpolis, 62, 115, 117
Hilprecht, 56
Hincks, 17, 19, 21, 22, 23, 25, 31, 161, 162
Hittite, 34; art, 180 et seq.; chiefs, 197; dirk, 65; inscriptions, 195; kings, vi., 175; language, 34, 174, 176, 200; mercenaries, 177, 193, 196, etc.; pottery, vi., 63, 149, 178, 179, 206
Hittites, 169, 170, 173, 174, 179, 194, etc., 206

Hommel, 105, 106, 116, 120
Horus, followers of, 61, 110, 123, 124
Hut-urns, 171
Hyksos, 52, 145, 156, 190; introduce bronze, 63; axe-heads, 171

In-Susinak, 50
Iron, name of, 58; in Armenia, 166; in Egypt, 62
Isaac, 154
Israelites, their advent in Canaan 212
Istar, 52, 128, 129, 153
Ivories of Ephesus, 184

Jacob-el (see Ya'qub-el), 145, 190
Jebusites, 205, 213
Jehu, 21
Jensen, 34, 168
Jéquier, 121
Jerusalem, 21, 178, 201, 205, 210, 213; king of, 196, 199, etc., 202, 204
Jones, F., 24

Kadish, 197, 208
Kara Eyuk, 47, 48, 53, 166, 169, 170, 171, 173, 181
Karnak, 54
Kas, 195, 201, 202
Kassites, 89; dynasty of, 97
Khabiri, 196, 201, 202
Khaldis, Khaldian, 164, 165
Khammu-rabi (see Amraphel), 81, 127, 143, 152, 157; code of laws of, 153; dynasty of, 155, 156, 167; letters of, 45
Khattinâ (Hittites), 202
Khorsabad, 18, 19
King, L. W., 40
Knossus, clay tablets at, 183
Knudtzon, 174, 196, 200
Kossæans (Kassites), 35, 144
Kretan script, 141, 159, 181; pottery, 178; monsters in art, 180
Krete, 141, 182
Kûyunjik, 18, 131. See Nineveh.

220 INDEX

THE CUNEIFORM INSCRIPTIONS

ASSYRIAN PRIMER AND ASSYRIAN TEXTS. An Inductive Method of Learning the Cuneiform Characters and Reading the Inscriptions. *J. Dyneley Prince, Ph.D. & Ernest A. Budge, M.R.A.S.*
ISBN 0-89005-226-3. viii + 60 + vi + 44pp. $12.50
The first edition combining in one volume Prince's *Assyrian Primer* (New York 1909) and Budge's *Assyrian Texts* (London 1880). The user of this new volume not only benefits from Prince's methodical introduction to the cuneiform writing (complete list of signs and many exercises) and his easy grammar of the Assyrian language, but also is given the opportunity to test his reading ability on the texts of the Royal Assyrian Inscriptions selected as readings by Budge. One of the best introductions available to Assyrian Cuneiform Epigraphy.

THE ARCHAEOLOGY OF THE CUNEIFORM INSCRIPTIONS. *A.H. Sayce, Professor of Assyriology, Oxford.*
ISBN 0-89005-228-X, vi + 220pp. + 16pl. $15.00
The mystery of the 'cuneiform' characters and the thousands of inscriptions written in them, was one of the fields of research in which the young men of science of archaeology realized one of its first victories. The task of deciphering the cuneiform writing was gradually accomplished by a group of dedicated scholars who first read the old Persian texts, then the Elamite and then finally the Babylonian and Assyrian documents.
Sayce, one of the leading scholars in Assyriology, narrates the story of the discoveries and then the decipherment in a real superb book considered a classic work in its kind. (R 1907).

SYRIA AND EGYPT. From the Tell El Amarna Letters. *W.M. Flinders Petrie.*
ISBN 0-89005-234-4, viii + 187pp. $12.50
During the age of the decline of Egyptian power in Syria, when the great conquests of Tahutmes I were all gradually lost, a splendid store of information was laid by for us in the cuneiform correspondence at Tell el Amarna. The clay tablets, mostly from Syria, but with a few duplicates of letters from Egypt, were deposited in "The place of the records of the palace of the king," as it is called upon the stamped bricks which I found still remaining there.
It is now the breaking up of all this power that we have detailed before us in the letters from Tell el Amarna. Much had been already lost in the later years of Amenhotep III; in letters 111, 112 the governor of Qatna near Damascus states that Azira, the centre of North Syrian independence, was in revolt, the Khatti were at war, and places round Damascus were rebelling. Yet up to the close of the reign of the third Amenhotep and beginning of the fourth, the letters passed regularly to and from Babylonia and northern Mesopotamia, so that no serious break of communications had taken place. The serious overthrow belongs to the reign of Akhenaten, when, having openly broken with all the traditions of his Amenhotep youth, he threw all his energies into domestic reform and abandoned foreign politics with disastrous results." From the *Introduction* by W.M. Flinders Petrie.

BIBLIOTHECA AEGYPTIACA

ARES PUBLISHERS presents for the first time a new program of reprinting at LOW BUDGET PRICES all the most important works on the LANGUAGE, HISTORY and CIVILIZATION of the ANCIENT EGYPTIANS. The volumes listed below ARE ALL AVAILABLE and you may order them directly from us (ALL PREPAID ORDERS mailed in 48 hours from receipt), or from your bookseller or book supplier.

ANCIENT EGYPTIAN MEDICINE: THE PAPYRUS EBERS. *Cyril Bryan.*
All sorts of remedies for ailments still plaguing the human race in this original work on ancient Egyptian medicine, as written by an ancient physician. The best information source known on Egyptian medical practices.
ISBN 0-89005-004-X. 208pp. $10.00

EGYPTIAN LANGUAGE: EASY LESSONS IN EGYPTIAN HIEROGLYPHICS.
E.A. Wallis Budge.
An easy introduction to the study of the ancient Egyptian language and hieroglyphic inscriptions. A lengthy list of hieroglyphic characters, telling both their value as idiograms and as phonetics. Shows how to decipher the ancient hieroglyphics.
ISBN 0-89005-095-3 .... $10.00
Student edition $6.00

EGYPTIAN HIEROGLYPHIC GRAMMAR: With Vocabularies, Exercises, Chrestomathy (A First Reader) Sign-List and Glossary. *S.A.B. Mercer.*
Mercer's grammar was a product of his experience in teaching Oriental Languages. His basic idea in writing was that "the beginner needs a textbook which is both simple and a so supplied with exercises" and that "the larger grammars are reference books and unsuited for the use of beginners."
Mercer divided his 'Grammar' into chapters or lessons, and supplied each chapter with copious exercises. He supplied also a fine selection of hieroglyphic texts forming a reader for the student, added a Sign-List with explanations of the signs and finally a Glossary translating the Egyptian words in English.
For the student who wishes to learn how to read and write the hieroglyphics and understand also the words and sentences formed by them, Mercer's book is an invaluable help.
ISBN 0-89005-203-4, viii + 184pp. $12.50

CATALOGUE OF THE EGYPTIAN HIEROGLYPHIC PRINTING TYPE.
Alan H. Gardiner.

An amazing collection of tables which provide instant identification of all the Egyptian hieroglyphs. Arranged by type, such as "Gods," "Goddesses," "Birds," "Parts of Animals," a glance at the index shows exactly where to find the hieroglyphs which you wish to decipher. Useful introductory section and listing of Egyptian alphabet.

ISBN 0-89005-098-8 .... **$6.00**

EGYPTIAN READINGBOOK: Exercises and Middle Egyptian Texts. *Selected & Edited by Dr. A. De Buck.*

The Egyptian Readingbook, compiled by one of the best Egyptologists of the University of Leyden, is a unique collection of literary, religious, and private texts written in hieroglyphics. The student who has worked with Budge's, *Egyptian Language* or Mercer's *Grammar* needs the texts in the 'Readingbook' for study and practice.

ISBN 0-89005-213-1. 220pp. 8½ x 11 .... **$20.00**

PAPER AND BOOKS IN ANCIENT EGYPT. *J. Cerny.*

The revolution that the invention of the book brought to the cultures of the ancient people of the Near-East and the Mediterranean started in Egypt. It was under the shade of the Megalithic Egyptian temples, that the first 'papyrus scroll' was developed and in the great libraries of the Ptolemaic period that the idea of the 'papyrus codex' was born many centuries later. Without the Egyptian thought and thinkers, writing could still be limited to materials that could have delayed considerably the expansion of information, education and learning.

Prof. Cerny's account of 'Paper and Books in Ancient Egypt,' is the most complete, documented and dependable study available. In its compact form, it contains more information and facts than any other reference work on the subject.

ISBN 0-89005-205-0, 37pp. **$5.00**

TEN YEARS DIGGING IN EGYPT. *Flinders Petrie.*

A most fascinating account by the premier Egyptologist describing some of the most important discoveries in Egypt at the end of the 19th century. Illustrated with the drawings of the author.

ISBN 0-89005-107-0. 250pp. **$10.00**

Student edition **$6.00**

HISTORICAL SCARABS. *Flinders Petrie.*

The pocket handbook for the historian and collector of scarabs, with original drawings by Petrie. A useful primer to Newberry's *Ancient Egyptian Scarabs*. Includes 69 plates.

ISBN 0-89005-122-4. 84pp. **$10.00**

Student edition **$6.00**

ANCIENT EGYPTIAN SCARABS. *P. Newberry.*

A concise work covering all aspects of scarabs, cylinder seals, signet rings and other seals used by the ancient Egyptian. Indispensable reference work for scholars and collectors.

ISBN 0-89005-092-9 . . . . *$10.00*

Student edition $6.00

CULTS AND CREEDS IN GRAECO-ROMAN EGYPT. *H. Idris Bell.*

Valuable information from ancient papyri on the previously confused history of the religions and cults of Graeco-Roman Egypt. Special selections on the pagan amalgam, Jews in Egypt and the rise of Christianity.

ISBN 0-89005-088-0. x + 117pp. *$10.00*

Student edition $6.00

INSCRIPTIONES GRAECAE AEGYPTI: INSCRIPTIONES NUNC CAIRO IN MUSEO. *G. Milne.*

The Greek inscriptions of Egypt included in this volume, originally published in the *Catalogue General des Antiquities Egyptiennes du Musee du Caire*, are here for the first time technically incorporated in the *Inscriptiones Graecae* along with the author's excellent commentaries.

ISBN 0-89005-111-9. 169pp. *$25.00*

INSCRIPTIONES GRAECAE PTOLEMAICAE I. *Max L. Strack.*

The first collection of Ptolemaic inscriptions not limited to the political boundaries of the Empire, but including inscriptions from all areas which came under the radiating influence of its culture. Also appearing is an appendix which includes tables for the "Names and Epithets of the Kings," his "Chronological List of the Kings," plus several commentaries.

ISBN 0-89005-171-2. 120pp. *$10.00*

The new series of the BIBLIOTHECA AEGYPTIACA is only a part of our publishing program of reprinting and publishing new books on the ANCIENT WORLD. Our 1977 catalogue lists more than 150 books in this special area, with emphasis on the ANCIENT NEAR EAST, the ANCIENT MEDITERRANEAN, ANCIENT GREECE, the HELLENISTIC WORLD and the WORLD OF ROME. If you are interested, send us a postcard with your name and address. We will mail to you a FREE copy.

ARES PUBLISHERS Inc.

612 NORTH MICHIGAN AVE., SUITE 216
CHICAGO, ILLINOIS 60611